W9-BFW-007

AN INSIDER'S LOOK AT THE NEW HIGH-FREQUENCY PHENOMENON THAT IS TRANSFORMING THE INVESTING WORLD

EDGAR PEREZ

NEW YORK CHICAGO SAN FRANCISCO LISBON LONDON
MADRID MEXICO CITY MILAN NEW DELHI SAN JUAN
SEOUL SINGAPORE SYDNEY TORONTO

The McGraw·Hill Companies

1 2 3 4 5 6 7 8 9 10 DOC/DOC 1 6 5 4 3 2 1

ISBN: 978-0-07-176828-3
MHID: 0-07-176828-9

e-ISBN: 978-0-07-176830-6
e-MHID: 0-07-176830-0

Library of Congress Cataloging-in-Publication Data

Perez, Edgar.
The speed traders : an insider's look at the new high-frequency phenomenon that is transforming the investing world / by Edgar Perez.
p. cm.
Includes bibliographical references and index.
ISBN 978-0-07-176828-3 (alk. paper)
1. Electronic trading of securities. 2. Investment analysis. 3. Portfolio management. I. Title.
HG4515.95.P37 2011
332.64'2—dc22 2011008769

This book is printed on acid-free paper.

Contents

Acknowledgments

This book is the result of many months of thinking, networking, and interviewing top high-frequency traders. I was drawn to high-frequency trading initially by my personal discovery that the financial markets were changing in an irreversible way. Precisely because of widespread misunderstanding of the practice, it occurred to me that a book featuring real people like you and me, with the same alpha-generation concerns that any other manager might have, would be an appropriate way to bridge the gap.

I would like to gratefully acknowledge the willing participation and helpful insights of the interviewees, whose comments appear liberally throughout the book, Adam Afshar, Aaron Lebovitz, Manoj Narang, John Netto, Stuart Theakston, and Peter van Kleef. Every day they are breaking new ground and expanding the frontiers of high-frequency trading.

Writing this book would not have been possible without the continuous interaction I have had with practitioners, quants, managers, academics, journalists, consultants, and investors in many networking receptions I have hosted in the last years. I particularly would like to acknowledge the speakers, panelists, and attendees at my High-Frequency Trading Happy Hour receptions, Experts and Leaders Forums, and Experts Workshops in New York, Hong Kong, Sydney, Singapore, Mumbai, Shanghai, and Beijing.

I owe particular thanks to Stephanie Frerich, Joseph Berkowitz, Daina Penikas, and the entire staff of McGraw-Hill, who had the vision to see this book as a contribution both to the practice and to the public debate. In addition, I would like to thank my teammates at Golden Networking, who have continually challenged me and helped me to come to new insights as we have grappled with this topic in recent years. Special thanks go to Mo Chen, Wesam Ahmed, Pavel Lubic, Jessica Ye, Sarah Gruber, and Roger Gu.

Finally, eternal thanks to my parents, Felipe and Saturnina, for their dedication, responsibility, and encouragement, and to my brother, Guido, for being so loyal and supportive.

Introduction

There was a time when investors all over the world were satisfied with holding periods that could have lasted a lifetime; indeed, there was this utopian view that stocks were on a path of ever-increasing prices, with occasional bumps on the way, as in the crisis of 1987. Jeremy Siegel's *Stocks for the Long Run* (McGraw-Hill, 2007) exemplified this notion of eternal and magical growth that engulfed investors big and small. Welcome to a world where every *micro*second counts.

This book will provide readers with a comprehensive review of the evolution of high-frequency trading through the most important events that marked its growth from Nasdaq's founding in the early 1970s to the "flash crash" of May 6, 2010, seasoned with first-account insights from successful practitioners and experienced experts. Six practitioners, either founders, chief executive officers, presidents, or managing directors at their funds, have been interviewed in depth on a range of topics, including their educational background, their introduction to the financial world, their initial involvement with high-frequency trading, and how they are succeeding in today's financial markets.

Before we get into this fascinating world, let's start off with an overview of high-frequency trading, reviewing practitioners' thoughts on an appropriate definition of this practice, its emergence in the United States and the rest of the world, the ever-important technology question of build versus buy, how profitable it really can be, the human component, and its impact on retail and institutional investors. Finally, we will walk through the definition of terms that sometimes get used incorrectly when describing high-frequency trading.

Definition of High-Frequency Trading

High-frequency trading is a term that has grown to encompass a diverse number of strategies that share only a few traits. Asked for a definition, interviewees offered many different versions, and many more can be found in other literature on the topic.

That being said, there are some common themes among the various high-frequency trading strategies. Execution speed and therefore latency are important factors in high-frequency trading. Whereas seconds might have been considered high-frequency trading until not so long ago, now practitioners talk about milliseconds and microseconds as minimum speeds of execution for latency-sensitive strategies, speeds that typically can be experienced by those trading in Nasdaq OMX exchanges. Therefore, computers play an important role in replacing slow humans in the trading decisions.

Turnover is another important characteristic. Most practitioners turn their holdings over quite often as opposed to traditional fund managers; since the profits per transaction are small, the only way to compensate for their heavy investment in infrastructure is through the transaction of hundreds of thousands of shares. That is why exchanges battle to accommodate thousands of trades per second, because no high-frequency trader would like to face capacity constraints when dealing with an exchange.

Finally, practitioners are used to maintaining minimal or nonexistent overnight positions. High-frequency traders are profitable when they are transacting, either through the small alpha of each transaction or potential rebates from the exchange; therefore, it doesn't make sense for them to maintain any holdings overnight;

as soon as they enter into a position, they try to profit from it and just as quickly get out. To be considered high frequency, what would the rate of turnover need to be? "Anything less than a day but typically more like a few minutes to a couple of hours," says Manoj Narang, CEO of Tradeworx. "In practical terms," he adds, "firms that run high-frequency strategies tend to finish the day with no stock holdings whatsoever." Because this characteristic mathematically implies a rate of turnover of more than once per day and is much simpler and less arbitrary than focusing on a particular holding period, it is a perfectly good definition of a high-frequency strategy on its own. Thus Narang proposes this definition: A high-frequency strategy is a strategy that seeks to unwind all positions so that the trader can go home "flat" at the end of each trading day.

Ultimately, says Andrew Kumiega, director of quality at Infinium Capital Management, the goal of any high-frequency trading firm is to have a portfolio of uncorrelated trading strategies. "They can be built uncorrelated even by trading the same instrument over different time frames. So you can diversify your portfolio of algorithms by instrument, by market, by time frame, by algorithm, and hopefully if you have enough of those, obtain sufficient returns to cover your operating cost with very narrow risk distribution. Another option is working not only algorithms but also projects. Think about this: each new algorithm goes through developmental stages. You don't know if your algorithm is going to work in stage 1; you really don't know until you are at stage 2 ([or perhaps] stage 3) whether what you build will work. Thus you have a real option of building an algorithm. And the same diversification principle applies; you would want a bunch of algorithms in a pipeline."[1]

Erik Lehtis, president of DynamicFX Consulting, explains the following defining characteristics of high-frequency trading: automation without any human intervention, employment of a certain finite amount of capital, and profit maximization by turning over positions enough that one essentially could have as much exposure to market risk or value as one's capital would allow if one were just taking a position or holding it all day long. He says: "You are using systems to manage your risk, keep track of your positions, and calculate your P&L [Profit and Loss]. If you are doing all these things, you are, by definition, a high-frequency trader. It is not a matter of what your holding period is, if it is milliseconds or microseconds; there is no hard and fast definition. But you will be turning over your inventory several times, if not hundreds of times, every day."[2]

For Richard Flom, vice president of trading for Systematic Alpha Management, high-frequency trading is systematic, algorithmic, and data-intensive: "I think it is important to mention that [it] applies to the three types of high-frequency traders: people who make markets looking at the order book, high-frequency traders that trade in reversion, and high-frequency traders that look at trends. It does not matter how long your holding period is, but it matters what your strategy is, and that's as robustly as I can put it."[3]

Lastly, Andrew Kumiega thinks that there is no conclusive definition: "Ben Van Vliet, a colleague at the Illinois Institute of Technology, and I worked together for 10 years, writing papers and books on the topic; we have 30 consulting engagements together. We still could not define what high-frequency trading is. High-frequency trading means everything to everyone. To some people it's microseconds. Some people are executing stocks; some people are hedging."

The Emergence of High-Frequency Trading

For many people, high-frequency trading is a recent phenomenon in the markets. By now, you must have noticed that the industry didn't grow overnight but over the course of the last decade or so, with a dramatic increase in the volume of electronic trading in the last five years. While there were many developments prior to that, the starting point was around 2000, as soon as electronic mechanisms were invented to access exchanges, says Flom.

Flom thinks that we have just seen the beginning of electronic trading; it is indeed an evolution, and it's just coming around in the last few years. What algorithmic traders have done over the last few years is learn from their exchanges how to execute on them. High-frequency trading, says Flom, is not something that everyone just starting up can do.

"It is something that you can stumble upon and then becomes very difficult for you right away, and it is something that is a growing process," says Flom. "You have to learn how to do it, and it is not always profitable. In the last few years, there have been shops that have been successful at doing trading algorithmically, and there have been many shops that were not successful at all and went out of business. Moving forward, I think that we will see more automation in the market; people are realizing that there are more market strategies that you can apply algorithms to. So that is one of the trends that we see. Another trend is that more exchanges are becoming accessible via electronic means. And as more people get involved in trading, more and more exchanges will take place."

Lehtis remembers his beginnings in the industry: "I first got involved around 2003. There was already high-frequency trading as a process. At that time, you could get involved even if you were not perfect. You could have some success, learn from your mistakes, and get positive feedback through your returns. And you could fine-tune your algorithm and do all the work necessary to basically patch up your performance based on the outcomes that you had. I think now, coming into this space raw with a clean slate, attempting to build a high-frequency trading arbitrage strategy, that it is a very challenging thing to do because you are not going to get the same kind of feedback. Even if you do 90 out of a 100 things right, you still will end up with negative returns because of the one thing that you didn't think of, and you are going to have a very hard time identifying it. So I don't envy anyone coming in now for the first time. I'm not saying it can't be done now, but it is a much more expensive proposition."

Looking forward, Lehtis says, "We will be dealing with much more perfect markets. Volatility and liquidity I think can have a very inverse relationship. The more you have of one, the less you have of the other. And right now we have a lot of volatility. But liquidity will return to the market and will give us some certainty as far as what we're doing. If the market feels at equilibrium, you won't be able to do these kinds of trades. Anything that is predictive, seeking alpha, I think those trades will be very interesting. Being able to model behavior on the fly, knowing where the market is going with some kind of certainty, that's where I'm most fascinated by the future of high-frequency trading. You want to be able to identify those moments where the market is about to turn, where that possibility is there, and be the first one to really start hitting the bid."

Paramount to the rapid evolution of high-frequency trading has been the fact that the United States has what is probably the world's most efficient equity market, says Petter Kolm, director of the mathematics in finance MS program at the Courant Institute of Mathematical Sciences of New York University. "That is for a number of different reasons. One is because of the great competition that we have in the intermarkets, and here I am not necessarily just talking about the participants, but I am also talking about the various trading venues that are competing. I mean, we have about 40 open equity trading venues in this country and, depending on how you count, probably about other 30 or so dark trading venues. And the major part of the liquidity provided in these trading venues is from what we classically refer to as the market makers. However, we no longer see these guys running around on the floor, unless we look at some of the pits in Chicago. Instead, the market makers have been replaced by computer algorithms. That is technological innovation."[4]

Even at this stage, Kolm admits that there is a certain level of fear among institutional investors and others, which happens with any new technology. "It takes a little bit of time to understand and absorb that," he says. "We can see that time and time again; when we look at history, when the first cars came out, it was exactly the same kind of debacle in the media. I wasn't around at that time, but I am sure it was pretty close to what we are seeing today. So I do think that one of the problems here is that there is a lack of information and a lack of education, and I can say that as an academic because that is what we are trying to change here. And over time, people will understand better what [high-frequency trading] is all about."

Is There a Place for Outsourcing in High-Frequency Trading?

In a recent poll released by Thomson Reuters of 100 New York–based representatives of hedge funds, proprietary traders, and broker-dealers, 50 percent of the participants stated that outsourcing parts of their high-frequency trading infrastructure would allow them to focus on higher-value-added activities and leverage their competitive advantages. Lehtis recommends that traders ask themselves what is it that they bring to the table that will make them successful in a way that other people are not and how are they going to compete with all the really smart people who are already in the space.

"There are a lot of people in this space already, regardless of what your assets are and what your time frames are," says Lehtis.

"Any algorithm that you might think of, other people are running it as well. So what makes you so sure that you are going to be successful? That is the sort of thing that you want to spend your energy and resources on in-house. Anything else that has been done before, you can buy it. You will save yourself a lot of time and headaches by not trying to reinvent the wheel. There are so many moving parts in a high-frequency trading system, so many components involved. You can build them, but you could spend an entire lifetime building and never be satisfied with the result." Traders might be looking for components to keep track of their risk, [but] those components have been developed so many times before [that it would be a waste of time for traders to develop those things themselves]." Lehtis says: "If that is the thing you think makes you special, then you are probably in the wrong business. Reduce everything to those trading components that you think are unique, and buy everything else. You'll save yourself a ton of time and money actually, believe it or not."

For Flom, the decision to outsource, difficult by nature, becomes more complex when traders realize they have to make a decision for each individual strategy. Traders will have to decide whether they want everyone to have access to it and have it outsourced, or whether they want it to be something that they keep in-house. Some of the easiest things to outsource are just the trading platforms that they are trading through, because those things are programmable and can be executed quite easily. It really takes a lot of development to come up with a proprietary trading platform, cautions Flom: "In the sense of gathering data and applying algorithms to it, you can outsource where you get your data from. But when you have the data and you want to apply the strategy to it, there is very little you can outsource because you have to have some secret or some knowledge about what you are doing to develop these strategies. So there are electronic procedures you can outsource, but in terms of your strategy, it is important to keep those things within the firm."

How Profitable Is High-Frequency Trading?

Throughout this book, the traders and I will be referring to an article that appeared in the print edition of the *New York Times* on July 24, 2009.[5] Several people attribute the popularity of high-frequency trading to the claims the article made. One of them was that high-frequency traders had generated $21 billion in profits in 2008. This number was put into question by Manoj Narang and many other high-frequency traders, who argued that the number was totally out of range. In fact, Narang estimates that high-frequency trading in U.S. equities generates annual profits of $2 billion to $3 billion. With this mind, what can be said about the profitability of high-frequency trading?

John Netto, founder and president of M3 Capital, sees two ways to consider profitability in high-frequency trading: "There is profitability from a business development standpoint, whereas one develops a strategy that is extremely scalable and can manage a number of assets even if it doesn't have the best returns. Then there is, of course, a strategy that can generate great returns but may face capacity constraints. At M3 Capital, we focus on developing both, because ultimately you want to be have a broadly diversified portfolio of noncorrelated quantitative strategies that takes into account a number of variables in the market."

For Netto, in terms of high-frequency trading with a homogeneous sledge hammer or based on purely speed products, that market is largely, if not yet completely, dead. He thinks that there still might be some opportunities outside the United States for those who access the markets there. But in terms of triangular arbitrage strategies that involve multiple currency products or in terms of developing new models, he still sees a lot of opportunity.

In this regard, he thinks that the biggest threat in terms of what can make high-frequency trading difficult is volatility compression: "High-frequency trading, or at least algorithmic trading, is predicated on price recovery, and volatility compression makes price recovery a much greater hindrance. The opportunity to make markets, provide liquidity, at least from some of the strategies that we are talking about, is much greater. So the opportunities that exist, whether they are discerned algorithmically, via discretion, or via an approach that is somewhere between those two lines really plays on what the market environment is, what the microstructures are, and how you as an opportunist can attack those venues."

There is a big issue with the more alpha-generating strategies at the ultra-high-frequency trading level, the market-making type of strategies. For Kolm, these are capacity constrained: "The hit rate is going to be a function of the number of people trading these strategies. So that is clearly capacity constrained, and that is the space we talk about. It is not about being fast; it is about being first, because, if you are faster than everyone else, you are the first one who can change your limit or the buys and sells at market moves, and you are also always going to be at the top of the book and have an opportunity to trade and make liquidity and thereby make the bid-ask rate and the associated rebate. So yes, there are capacity constraints, something we discussed during the turmoil in the markets of August 2007 and the quant turmoil, where people were trading fact-based strategies, and everyone realized that we were all trading exactly the same strategies here (at least on that particular day everyone was correlated). However, I don't think it is something that we should have to worry so much about; we knew all that already when we got into that."

Ultimately, concludes Peter van Kleef, CEO of Lakeview Arbitrage, the most profitable high-frequency trading strategies generally are the ones that are not well publicized and occur where people do things differently than the rest of the crowd.

The Human Element in High-Frequency Trading

There are different opinions among my interviewees about human participation in the trading activities. Whereas some, such as Adam Afshar, suggest that humans should be completely removed from the trading process, others like to use the analogy of race cars or airplanes. Flom explains: "Race cars have been evolving over the last 10, 20, or 30 years, yet you still need someone behind the wheel. You can put an airplane on autopilot, but you still need someone behind the wheel to land it or take off. I think traders need to constantly be vigilant and to understand the risk and the algorithms they are trading. Traders can't just look at a model and say that it isn't working anymore; there is a constant pressure to be ahead of the game and understand what these algorithms are trading, to make sure that these algorithms are doing exactly what the researchers are expecting them to be doing, and giving them constant feedback, to the quants, researchers, and portfolio managers, about evolving strategies."

Traders are the eyes, the people who are watching these markets and algorithms, contends Flom. The algorithms are very sophisticated, and these people need to be there. "I think we could all agree that if we locked up an algorithm and let it trade on its own for 10 minutes, we would find that a lot of things will go wrong," he says. "Traders need to constantly monitor all the executions that are happening, give feedback, and provide all kinds of information back to research. Quants are sometimes just developing a model and putting it in trading; they never get to know how the model is doing. Sometimes there is nothing wrong with the model, even if it doesn't work; sometimes it just needs to be tweaked. So they need to understand what these algorithms are, what they are trading, and why they are trading them and give continuous feedback as well as monitor all the risk that is involved in these systems."

For Lehtis, traders have to be very involved in the technology because they have to be able to perform an autopsy on a bad trade: "They have to be able to decide what's wrong. The problem is that we usually only respond to positive feedback. But sometimes you are making money for the wrong reasons, and it certainly could cost you in the future."

High-Frequency Trading in the United States and the World

High-frequency trading started in the United States and continues to thrive here, according to James Leman, principal of Westwater Corp. He attributes this to the fact that the U.S. market is the optimal market right now for a lot of this type of trading. Ultimately, he adds, what matters is what traders are saying in terms of business opportunities, revenue opportunities, and the kinds of asset classes that traders are going after.

Despite the expansion of high-frequency trading around the world, the U.S. market is the one that gets talked about most in the trading community and also the one, with Europe, that is attracting more regulatory attention. As Leman says: "We need to pay attention to regulatory changes that are coming in the United States and probably should be in some level of motion in the European community. Naked access is the favorite poster child for what certain brokers allow certain high-frequency traders to do. There is a new rule in front of the Securities and Exchange Commission [SEC] that is being considered, talking about how brokers are going to have absolute responsibility for entitling buy-side customers to use their systems to get to the market; that would require documented procedures and the management of the company to sign off the annual review of how this takes place. The thought is that there is going to be essentially real-time risk controls imposed on high-frequency traders by brokers that give access to these electronic marketplaces, whether they are exchanges or ATSs [Alternative Trading Systems]."

Important components of markets that allow high-frequency trading include small minimum price variations, small transaction sizes, and automatic execution. It all comes down to speed, though. According to Leman: "Ever since Regulation NMS went into effect, things also have become much more intense because you can't get around it. High-frequency traders, because of the speed issue, are trying to get to the top of the book and hit the market as quickly as possible; that's the name of the game, especially for the market-making guys as opposed to the risk-arbitrage-oriented people. So low latency is very important, and we obviously all know we have gone from milliseconds now into microseconds, so a number of people now are quantifying things in 100 microseconds or below. Exchanges are talking about it because they are competing with one another in terms of speed, broker-dealers are competing with one another in terms of speed, and third-party vendors are competing with one another in terms of speed, so speed is essential."

The maker/taker pricing mechanism is important too; for market makers, the opportunity to earn the rebate along with the spread they pick up on doing the trading is the reason they are in the game; because of the transactions' very minimal size, there's a pressing need for high volumes of trading. Leman cites a recent statistic that looks at the number of orders versus the number of messages that go on; just one order to 30 messages that are going on canceling and replacing, canceling and replacing. That's why ultrahigh speed is very important and we see the Singapore exchange reducing its time to execute trades from between 3 and 5 milliseconds to 90 microseconds, the fastest in the world.

Looking at the different elements that are necessary for high-frequency opportunities to really exist, the U.S. equities market has just about all of them. Says Leman: "U.S.-listed options, Canadian equities, and a number of European markets also have essentially all the components but maybe not some of the speed issues, maybe not the maker/taker component, and maybe not some of the automatic execution mechanisms. Listed futures, foreign exchange, and other international markets are also developing."

When Leman first got started in electronic trading, it seemed that the equity market in the United States was the poster child for how things were going to eventually follow out of the world. He was around at the New York Stock Exchange when it created the DOT [Designated Order Turnaround] system, and then the exchange started putting customer electronic trading on desks, first in the United States and later in Asia. Leman's team helped to develop the Financial Information eXchange (FIX) Protocol,[6] still the de facto messaging standard for pretrade and trade communication globally within the equity markets. "So now we are seeing a number of MTFs [Multilateral Trading Facilities] evolving in Europe along with the way ECNs [Electronic Communication Networks] and ATSs have evolved in the United States, and they are all now vying for things; we don't have a consolidated type in Europe, but a number of people are trying to bring pressure to make that happen. We are seeing that every market is probably going through the same evolution in order to attract the same kind of trading activity. In most markets that developed outside the United States, the speed issue probably will continue to pick up in terms of adoption; in other words, the marketplaces will adopt these technologies more quickly than their predecessors did."[7]

Money Managers and Institutional Investors as "Victims"?

Much has been said about high-frequency trading and traditional money managers and institutional investors as "victims" of this activity. Practitioners interviewed for this book don't see institutional investors in that way.

According to Kolm, institutional investors are already allocating capital to high-frequency trading strategies. "An important aspect of electronic trading for them is optimal execution. Executing large orders of shares is primarily a sell-side function being offered to institutional investors. I think this is a function that many of the large institutional investors want themselves to take charge of. That is the low-hanging fruit in electronic trading. And when people get comfortable with that, they look at what is the next branch, where is the next apple, and they will go a little bit higher up the tree. I think the institutional investors will get more and more comfortable with high-frequency strategies."

Van Vliet envisions a new dynamic in this regard: "If you look at each strategy like a business, it is not inconceivable that someone could spin off their high-frequency market-making business to a larger institutional investor. Is this going toward a utility type of thing where there are a few very large institutional liquidity providers running market-making styles, high-frequency trading style strategies that require a tremendous amount of information technology infrastructure? If you look at it like a business that generates revenue, I think certainly you see institutional investors."[8]

Lehtis agrees with Van Vliet's proposed scenario: "A few dominant players try to take over, they discover what the economies of scale are, they just make it a critical-mass game that very few other people can play, and then they start merging with each other, and before you know, it is a monopoly. There is no doubt about it. The cost of entry in the high-frequency trading space is enormous, especially in foreign exchange, but I think in any of the asset classes. There is so much knowledge you need, so much technology you need to invest in, and it is the support of the technology as well as the initial build and the capital that you have to have available. It is a nontrivial tribute, and as time goes by and these firms get better, they will, without a doubt, just naturally push out the smaller players. So, if you want the benefits of self-execution of these orders, and you are doing the smart writing yourself, rather than just receiving a price back from someone who did that for you, you have to be of a sufficient scale to make it economically worthwhile; otherwise, it just doesn't pay. So it is in the interest of the big firms to make that equation not work out to do it yourself but for you to execute orders through them."

While it is not surprising that most people haven't had the opportunity to learn about high-frequency trading in detail, it is surprising to see the range of opinions the practice elicits from traditional money managers, those who manage allocations from high-net-worth individuals to institutional investors.

Traditional value investors who follow the Graham-Dodd philosophy of investing don't seem to be bothered by high-frequency trading. Faithful to the investing discipline, they look for authentic value stocks that will perform positively over the long run; therefore, buying them at one or two more pennies wouldn't affect their performance. In fact, at one forum organized by Columbia Business School, alma mater of the greatest value investors, managers indicated that high-frequency trading had no impact whatsoever on their strategies.

Important Definitions

Finally, there is so much information (or misinformation, according to some) about high-frequency trading that's important to know, that this Introduction would be incomplete if I neglected to define certain terms that will be discussed throughout this book.

- **Program trading** is a generic term used to describe a type of trading in securities, usually consisting of baskets of stocks. It is loosely defined as an electronic transaction involving 15 or more stocks with a combined value of at least $1 million.

Three factors help to explain the explosion in program trading. First, technological advances spawned the growth of electronic communication networks (ECNs). These electronic exchanges, such as Instinet (later absorbed by Nasdaq OMX) and Archipelago (later absorbed by NYSE Euronext), allow thousands of buy and sell orders to be matched very rapidly without human intervention. Second, the SEC mandated in 2001 that the major stock exchanges price stocks in dollars and cents instead of fractions. A stock previously priced at 7⅛ is now listed at $7.13. Pricing stocks in penny increments instead of 1⁄16 increments results in 100 price points within a dollar instead of the previous eight price points. This means that all the willing buyers and sellers are dispersed over many more prices, making it more difficult for them to meet on price. Finally, perhaps most significantly, the proliferation of hedge funds with all their sophisticated trading strategies is driving program-trading volume.[9]

- **Quantitative trading** refers to strategies based on quantitative analysis, which relies on mathematical computations and number crunching to identify trading opportunities. Price and volume are two of the more common data inputs used in quantitative analysis as the main inputs to mathematical models. Since quantitative trading generally is used by financial institutions and hedge funds, the transactions usually are large in size and may involve the purchase and sale of hundreds of thousands of shares and other securities. However, quantitative trading is also commonly used by individual investors.

Quantitative trading techniques include high-frequency trading, algorithmic trading, and statistical arbitrage. Many individual investors are more familiar with quantitative tools such as moving averages and oscillators.[10]

- **Algorithmic trading** is about using a set of rules to finesse trade execution. Algorithmic trading involves splitting a trade into multiple orders in order to reduce visibility and market impact, but the decision to take the main trade might or might not be automated. A fund manager might decide that a particular stock looks attractive based on his or her fundamental analysis and then instruct his or her trading desk to buy a block of stock. The traders on the desk might well use trade-execution algorithms to finesse the placement of this trade.[11]
- **Automated trading** involves a set of rules (a very simple example might be a pair of moving averages of different lengths crossing over) that, when satisfied, automatically trigger the placement of an order. A small, simple automated trade might be placed directly into the market, whereas a more substantial one might be handed to an execution algorithm for placement in small order slices so as to reduce market impact, etc. In brief, an automated model determines *whether* to place a trade, whereas an algorithmic model determines *how* to place it.[12]
- **Proprietary trading** refers to the practice by which banks, brokerages, and other financial institutions trade on their own account rather than on behalf of a customer. In simple terms, proprietary, or prop, trading is where a trading desk, using the bank's own capital and balance sheet, carries out trades in various instruments, often for speculative purposes. They can be ordinary shares and bonds traded on exchanges but more often are derivatives—either exchange-traded or in the over-the-counter markets—or foreign exchange. So-called pure proprietary trading is where traders trade for the bank's own profit, unrelated to client business. These traders generally are "walled off" from the rest of the bank and generate only a portion of total trading revenues. The practice is being severely limited in the United States by the Volcker rule, a

provision of the Dodd-Frank financial-overhaul law that was intended to curb the ability of banks to take risks with their own capital.

The other type of trading banks do is to help clients carry out trades, where the desk will use the bank's own capital to make a market in a certain instrument, offering itself as a buyer to a client who wants to sell or a seller to a client who wants to buy. Known as *flow business*, this is not speculative trading by the banks. Yet, to a certain extent, it still puts the bank's own capital at risk, sometimes in as significant a way as if the bank were conducting its own speculative prop trading.[13]

- **Statistical arbitrage**, or *StatArb*, as opposed to (deterministic) arbitrage, is related to the statistical mispricing of one or more assets based on the expected value of these assets. For example, consider a game in which one flips a coin and collects \$1 on heads or pays 50 cents on tails. In any single flip, it is uncertain if one will win or lose money. However, in the statistical sense, there is an expected value of $\$1 \times 50\% - \$0.50 \times 50\% = \$0.25$ for each flip. According to the law of large numbers, the mean return on actual flips will approach this expected value as the number of flips increases. This is precisely the way in which a gambling casino makes a profit. In other words, statistical arbitrage conjectures statistical mispricings or price relationships that are true in expectation in the long run when repeating a trading strategy.

  As a trading strategy, statistical arbitrage is a heavily quantitative and computational approach to equity trading. It describes a variety of automated trading systems that commonly make use of data mining, statistical methods, and artificial intelligence techniques. A popular strategy is pairs trading, in which stocks are put into pairs by fundamental- or market-based similarities. When one stock in a pair outperforms the other, the poorer performing stock is bought long with the expectation that it will climb toward its outperforming partner; the other is sold short. This strategy hedges risk from whole-market movements.

In recent years, there has been a trend away from simple pair trading, and now it is more common for portfolios of stocks to be *clustered* by sector and region in offsetting any beta exposure. After the portfolio is constructed in this manner, it is usually optimized using risk models such as Barra/APT/EMA/Northfield to constrain or eliminate various risk factors.[14]

- **Ultra-high-frequency trading**, according to Telesis Capital's Rishi Narang, is a subcategory of high-frequency trading that is extremely sensitive to latency down to milliseconds and microseconds. "Most of the chatter out there now is really about ultra-high-frequency trading, when colocation really matters and shaving off milliseconds is important," he said. "It doesn't matter nearly as much for generic short-term quantitative trading."[15]

CHAPTER 1

The Emergence of High-Frequency Trading

While high-frequency trading has gained relevance with the general public only recently, the practice of using computerized trading has been active for decades, going as far back as 1971, when Nasdaq started as the world's first electronic market.

In the Beginning, 1969–1976

Traditionally, financial markets were physical locations where brokers with buying and selling orders met and matched them appropriately. The technological evolution and, consequentially, the exponential growth of computing power brought a revolution to the financial markets, making it unnecessary for brokers to meet physically and enabling traders from remote locations to participate. The now Nomura-owned Instinet led the charge more than three decades ago.

February 24, 1969

On this day, Institutional Networks Corp. filed a patent application for its "Instinet Communication System for Effectuating the Sale or Exchange of Fungible Properties Between Subscribers." The company, founded two years before, aimed to compete with the New York Stock Exchange by means of computer links between banks, mutual funds, and insurance companies, with no delays or intervening specialists. Through this Instinet system, which would start operating by 1970, the company would provide computer services and a communications network for the automated buying and selling of equity securities on an anonymous, confidential basis. It also acted as a securities information processor, supplying professional-level market data systems containing last sale, quote, and size information. Institutional Networks received income from commissions on the trades and from the rental of the Instinet terminals located in the offices of its clients. Institutional Networks was renamed Instinet in 1985.[1]

February 8, 1971

This was the first trading day at the Nasdaq, an electronic alternative to over-the-counter stock exchanges. Nasdaq opened electronically with 2,500 over-the-counter stocks. It was not until the 1990s that the Nasdaq became a competitor of the New York Stock Exchange (NYSE); Nasdaq merged with the American Stock Exchange (AMEX) in 1998.[2]

May 1, 1975

On this date, the Securities and Exchange Commission (SEC) banned fixed minimum commission rates, a cornerstone of the

U.S. securities markets and all other organized exchanges throughout the world.[3] "Until then, the NYSE fixed the minimum commission of stock trading; these extraordinary high costs had hindered quantitative traders from entering the equity markets,"[4] according to author Lars Kestner.

March 1, 1976

The fully automated Designated Order Turnaround (DOT) system was introduced on this day by the NYSE to route smaller orders electronically. The orders attended by a stock exchange agency would be sent electronically to the computers inside the market, allowing the stock exchange agencies to confirm the execution of some operations while still having the client on the telephone line,[5] significant progress for the time.

The DOT system involved the use of computer technology to relay orders. With a network interface, it was possible for investors to submit orders that were immediately logged in the servers for the exchange. The orders could be executed and confirmation of the execution relayed to the investor in what was then considered real time. This type of real-time investment capability made it possible for investors to benefit by having an order executed immediately rather than 10 minutes or an hour later. The DOT system was able to handle such transactions as limit orders, basket trades, and several other types of market orders.[6]

The Lead-up to Black Monday, 1982–1987

There were many voices eventually blaming the market collapse on electronic trading. The "flash crash" of 2010? No, Black Monday in 1987. That's right—even back then, startups and banks, which were just getting started in the electronic trading race, were pointed as the culprits of the dramatic decline in the financial markets. The story would repeat itself 23 years later.

July 5, 1984

On this date, the NYSE approved the use of a version of the Super-DOT system for options trading. Super-DOT was an improvement over the DOT system and guaranteed that any market order of less than 2,100 shares of a stock would be executed within three minutes at the prevailing bid price (for a market sell order) or asked price (for a market buy order) at the time the order was entered or at better prices, if possible.[7] The DOT-for-Options system provided the NYSE options floor with an electronic order-routing system not available on any other options exchange. The Super-DOT system, which included the NYSE's DOT, Opening Automated Report Service (OARS), and Limit Order (LMT), had been used to provide automated trading support to the NYSE equities trading floor since 1976.

October 19, 1987

After five days of intensifying stock market declines, selling pressure hit a peak on this day, Black Monday. The Dow Jones Industrial Average (DJIA) fell a record 22 percent, with many stocks halted during the day because order imbalances prevented true price discovery. The lead-up to October 1987 had seen the DJIA more than triple in five years, and price/earnings (P/E) multiples on stocks had reached above 20, implying very bullish sentiment. And while the crash began as a U.S. phenomenon, it quickly affected stock markets around the globe; 19 of the 20 largest markets in the world saw stock market declines of 20 percent or more.[8]

Floor traders, working by telephone, dominated the action, and computer-generated trading still was in its infancy; certainly, dark pools and high-frequency trading were the stuff of science fiction, said the *Wall Street Journal*. Nevertheless, that didn't stop people from speculating on the exact causes of the crash (which was rare in that the market made up most of its losses rather quickly rather than falling into a protracted economic recession) and pointing to automatic trading programs in place at the time as possible culprit. An important parallel, though, was how a number of traders abandoned the market; in 1987, some human market makers on the floor of the exchange stopped providing bids for certain stocks; more than two decades later, in a market dominated by technology, high-speed traders, who often provide liquidity for the market, just switched off their computers for very important reasons that will be detailed in Chapter 9.

Technology Improves, 1994–2001

Upstarts and established players jockeyed for positions at the end of the 1990s to advance their standing as the SEC readied itself to approve Regulation ATS, the regulation of alternative trading systems, an area now dominated by BATS (Better Alternative Trading System) and Direct Edge.

August 1, 1994

On this date, Banque Nationale de Paris (BNP) announced that it would purchase most of the operations of Cooper Neff, a Philadelphia-based options trading firm with a reported $400 million in capital, to provide a broader array of financial products to its corporate and institutional clients worldwide. The acquisition would include all of Cooper Neff's technology and research capabilities, as well as most of its trading operations.

Richard Cooper, founding partner of Cooper Neff, expected the buyout would push his firm "into the direct OTC [over-the-counter] customer market" using BNP's clients in Europe and Asia. Before, Cooper Neff's 100-plus traders made markets in exchange-traded options only and traded for the firm's own account. Later in the decade, Cooper Neff would become the largest program-trading firm in the United States.[9]

Cooper Neff was characterized in 1998 as another example of wizardry that worked. In an enlightening article in *BusinessWeek*, BNP/Cooper Neff was referred to as the firm focused on the arbitrage between stocks that had become overvalued or undervalued because of such things as money flows in and out of markets. The company was scrupulously neutral on the attractiveness of growth stocks versus cyclic stocks or large-cap stocks versus small-cap stocks. Although the firm's assets under management weren't huge, about $10 billion, it was estimated that it accounted for about 4 percent of the daily trading volume on the NYSE and 6 to 10 percent of the volume on the principal exchanges of France, Germany, Spain, and Italy. BNP/Cooper Neff, which was so far not open to outside investors, needed enormous volumes of trades because its average profit margin per trade was so small. Its research staff included about a dozen physics Ph.D.s. Contrary to what most funds would have claimed, chairman and cofounder Richard W. Cooper had said that August was the company's best month in history, pointing out that in markets that become irrational, you can find greater mispricing opportunities.[10]

December 4, 1994

On this date, William Christie and Paul Schultz, in a paper entitled, "Why Do Nasdaq Market Makers Avoid Odd-Eighth Quotes?" published by the *Journal of Finance*, pointed out that odd-eighths spreads were rare on Nasdaq because dealers rarely quoted prices ending in 1/8, 3/8, 5/8, and 7/8; therefore, the inside spread always was at least 1/4. Just the day after the study was reported in news, spreads suddenly narrowed, which was interpreted by the authors as evidence of tacit collusion. Ultimately, a federal class-action lawsuit against the Nasdaq won $1.03 billion in 1998.[11]

November 28, 1997

Xetra, an all-electronic trading system operated by Deutsche Börse, based in Frankfurt, Germany, was launched on this date. The Xetra platform offered increased flexibility for seeing order depth within the markets and trading in stocks, funds, bonds, warrants, and commodities contracts. The Xetra system was created originally for use on the Frankfurt Stock Exchange but has expanded to be used by various stock exchanges throughout Europe.[12] As a result of its plans to acquire NYSE Euronext, Deutsche Börse is now planning to merge Xetra cash equity market with the Euronext platform to form a pan-European share-trading market.

April 4, 1998

On this date, James and Marilyn Simons hosted a party at their Setauket home on Long Island for fellow mathematicians attending the "Connections in Modern Mathematics and Physics" meeting, a special geometry festival in honor of Simons on the occasion of his sixtieth birthday.[13] It was interesting to see that James Simons, founder of Renaissance Technologies, famous for shunning the limelight and rarely giving interviews to the press, opened his house for the occasion. Once, citing Benjamin the donkey in *Animal Farm*, he tried to explain his behavior: "God gave me a tail to keep off the flies, but I'd rather have had no tail and no flies."[14]

April 21, 1999

Regulation ATS, the regulation of alternative trading systems (ATSs), became effective on this day. The term *ATSs* was to encompass systems that the SEC previously had called *proprietary trading systems*, *broker-dealer trading systems*, and *electronic communications networks* (ECNs). In addition to a variety of reporting and operating requirements, there were three main elements to the new framework. First, the SEC adopted a new interpretation of key terms in the statutory definition of exchange to include ATSs performing market functions. Second, authority provided by Congress to exempt systems from exchange registration was invoked to give ATSs the option of registering as exchanges or as broker-dealers and complying with various requirements. Finally, the Securities Exchange Act of 1934 was interpreted to accommodate the registration of for-profit entities as exchanges.[15]

July 12, 1999

On this date, Goldman Sachs announced that it would buy Hull Group, Inc., a leading electronic trading company, for $531 million, making it one of the world's largest electronic market makers for derivatives, especially stock and index options. Goldman's purchase of Hull, its first major acquisition since becoming a public company two months before, was a calculated bet that people and institutions increasingly would buy and sell securities electronically rather than in private deals or on traditional exchange floors. Hull, which is based in Chicago and would operate as a subsidiary of Goldman, was one of the largest electronic traders and specialized in derivatives trading. Hull derived more than half its revenue from Europe, where electronic trading of securities was a step ahead of that in the United States, said M. Blair Hull, Hull's founder and chief executive. It had a substantial presence on stock exchanges in Britain, Germany, and France.

Like other large securities firms, Goldman had invested in new electronic securities exchanges, known as *electronic communications networks* (ECNs), that match buyers and sellers of stocks outside traditional exchanges such as the New York Stock Exchange and the Nasdaq. Such exchanges helped to fill buy and sell orders for less money and at all hours. They had already succeeded in taking some business away from the established exchanges.[16]

January 11, 2001

On this date, the SEC approved the Nasdaq stock market's SuperMontage plan to centralize display of its best stock quotes, overriding opposition from automated trading networks that compete with it. In granting Nasdaq the preliminary approval of the new system in January 2001, the SEC ordered it to create an alternative automated system for electronic trading networks that do not want to use it. Known as the Alternative Display Facility (ADF), the other system posted stock prices but didn't permit its users to execute trades.

Nasdaq screens would display only the single best buy and sell orders, so investors looking for the next-best quotes must search the ECNs. The ECNs, which automatically match buy and sell orders, accounted for about a third of Nasdaq's volume. ECNs, like Instinet from the Reuters Group, had expressed concern that they would lose business under the SuperMontage plan.[17]

Regulating the Market, 2001–2008

If there was a clear turning point for electronic trading, it arguably would be the decision by the SEC to require all U.S. exchanges to convert to decimals. Thereafter, it would just be a matter of time for ECNs and ATSs to experience explosive volume growth.

April 9, 2001

This was the deadline established by the SEC, the federal agency that oversees the U.S. stock markets, for all U.S. stock markets to convert to decimals. The decimal system brought several benefits to investors, according to NYSE chairman and CEO Richard A. Grasso. In June 2000, he had told a congressional committee that decimals would generate stockholder savings. Studies had shown that investors could save $1 billion or more a year. Stockholders would save on commissions paid to stockbrokers. Commissions often were based on the price of a share. Previously, stock prices had been measured in sixteenths of a dollar, or 6.25 cents. Now, price increases could be measured to the penny, making smaller fluctuations in price and smaller commissions possible. Since most other stock exchanges already used decimals, the United States would be more compatible with the rest of the world. Grasso also told the committee that the NYSE had upgraded its technology to handle twice as many transactions.[18]

June 10, 2002

On this date, Instinet announced plans to acquire competitor Island ECN. The move came just under two months before Nasdaq rolled out its beefed-up order and execution system known as SuperMontage, which had been engineered to provide the best liquidity for market makers big and small. While Instinet served 40 markets around the world, Nasdaq trades were the lion's share of its business. Island recently had made a name for itself as a marketplace for increasingly popular exchange-traded funds (ETFs).

Instinet and privately held Island were both ECNs that had garnered favor in the 1990s with institutional and professional traders looking for fast, cheap, and anonymous trade execution, a platform in which Nasdaq itself had fallen behind. Worth nearly $3.5 billion at the initial public offering (IPO), Instinet had watched its market share and market value shrink as lower trading volumes and decimalization made stock trading a less lucrative business.

Over the past year, Nasdaq had been slowing moving toward going public itself. Although it hadn't officially filed an IPO registration, the company had filed all other documents required for a public company with the SEC. The Nasdaq planned to use an IPO to increase its global scope, which included ventures in Japan and Europe, attempting to head off ECNs before their international market share swelled.[19]

August 28, 2002

On this date, the SEC approved Nasdaq's use of its new ATS, which cost the company more than $100 million to develop and had been stymied repeatedly by the lobbying efforts of its rapidly growing competitors; the system would let investors view orders placed through a variety of marketplaces that were then separate from one another. SEC officials said that they had sought to balance concerns raised by rivals about anticompetitive aspects of the system against the promise that it actually may lead to important advantages for investors.

The architects of the system said that by posting stock prices and orders from all market participants and rivals, the new system, known as SuperMontage, would enable stock traders to pick from a variety of sources for the lowest buy and highest sell prices.[20]

October 9, 2002

On this date, Tradebot Systems, Inc., for the first time traded 100 million shares in a single day, most of them stocks listed on the Nasdaq. The kind of trading practiced by Tradebot, founded by David Cummings, was a particularly fast form of *algorithmic* or *black-box trading*, in which computer programs decided when to buy and sell securities.

Cummings' strategy, which was shorter term than most and was highly reliant on speed, had been made possible by the growth of electronic trading networks. Electronic exchanges used computer systems to match buyers and sellers. They executed orders without involving floor traders known as *specialists*, who arrange transactions through auctions on the NYSE. For years, these specialists and the Wall Street dealers who traded Nasdaq stocks had profited on gaps between bid and offer prices.[21]

Hedge funds such as SAC Capital Advisors, D. E. Shaw & Co., and Renaissance Technologies had been using computers in their investment strategies for years. For example, computers were being programmed to take news headlines into account when executing trades, and media companies, including Dow Jones & Co., publisher of the *Wall Street Journal*, and Reuters Group, had begun releasing news in computer-readable formats that cater to them.

Despite these early offerings, the applicability of computers remained limited; Manoj Narang didn't think they were particularly relevant to high-frequency trading, although they had some possible implications for the broader field of algorithmic trading or statistical arbitrage. For Stuart Theakston, the extent to which machines could extract meaning from text-based information still was very limited and would remain so for some time. Aaron Lebovitz was more optimistic: "I think they [computers] will have a place in the long-run landscape; some startups are doing some really interesting things in this space, but the concept is very young and very complicated, and it may take a while to find its way." Ever the visionary, Peter van Kleef thought that social networking and news-based algorithms were definitely the next wave in things to come; however, the slow pickup suggested that most people were still struggling with the high-frequency trading basics and were not yet ready to move to the next levels.

December 4, 2002

On this date, the 104-year-old Chicago Mercantile Exchange (CME) was slated to go public. Analysts had said that the CME could follow the success of the Toronto Stock Exchange, the only exchange in North America to go public; it had seen its stock rise about 22 percent since its IPO in November 2002.

The CME was luring investors with its long track record (it had earned $68.3 million in 2001 and had been profitable in four of the past five years), the ability to profit from market swings (it was the number one domestic exchange for futures contracts, which allow investors to cut their risks by locking in prices for investments), and the small offering size (the CME was raising only an estimated $154.4 million by selling 4.8 million shares).[22]

December 4, 2003

Lakeview Arbitrage, a proprietary trading house specializing in statistical arbitrage, was incorporated on this date. Peter van Kleef, its founder, had managed significant hedge-fund-type investment portfolios and quantitative trading departments for, among others, Cooper Neff, Salomon Brothers, HypoVereinsbank, and Credit Lyonnais.[23]

May 26, 2004

On this date, the Nasdaq Stock Market, Inc., announced it had entered into a definitive agreement to acquire Brut, LLC, the owner and operator of the Brut ECN, for a total consideration of $190 million in cash from SunGard Data Systems, Inc. The board of directors of each company had approved the transaction, which was expected to close during the third quarter of 2004, subject to customary closing conditions and regulatory approval. The Brut acquisition was intended to enhance Nasdaq's systems by providing Nasdaq with the ability to route orders via an internal broker-dealer to multiple liquidity pools in keeping with changes proposed by Regulation NMS, as well as to improve FIX connectivity.[24]

April 20, 2005

On this date, the NYSE announced plans to merge with Archipelago Holdings, Inc., an all-electronic exchange founded in 1997. By tapping what NYSE CEO John Thain described as Archipelago's "high-speed, low-cost" all-electronic exchange, the NYSE would market a stock-listing alternative that would list companies that didn't qualify to go public on the NYSE on that date in order to compete directly with the Nasdaq Stock Market. It also would let the combined company offer new traded products beyond equities, including derivatives such as options (a business that Archipelago was already pursuing), corporate bonds, and other listed products. Archipelago Exchange would later be renamed NYSE Arca.

The NYSE had been slowly moving toward adding electronic trading by giving its floor-based trading specialists tools for what's referred to as *hybrid trading*. Thain had predicted that floor-based trading operations, where specialists make markets in particular stocks, would continue to be an important source of liquidity and trading volume. "The floor really does add value," he said.

Archipelago started as an ECN that provided an electronic platform through which traders could execute trades on stocks listed on Nasdaq and the NYSE. Such ECNs thrived in the day-trading boom and built their reputations on providing fast and transparent pricing information and trade executions. Archipelago became a stock exchange by joining with the Pacific Stock Exchange, and it went public in 2004.[25]

April 22, 2005

On this date, the Nasdaq agreed to buy Instinet Group, Inc., combining the two largest electronic markets for U.S. equities to form a stronger competitor to the NYSE.

The stakes for the Nasdaq, already high because it had lost business to newer electronic markets such as Instinet, escalated two days before, when the NYSE, the world's largest stock exchange, agreed to buy Archipelago Holdings, Inc. Both electronic exchanges and electronic trading systems known as ECNs can trade Nasdaq stocks.

Bloomberg LP competed with Reuters in providing news, information, and trading systems to the financial services industry. Bloomberg Tradebook competed with Instinet and Archipelago in the business of matching stock trade orders.

Instinet had been founded in 1969, two years before the National Association of Securities Dealers (NASD) created the

Nasdaq electronic market. Instinet was a wholly owned subsidiary of Reuters from May 1987 until its IPO in May 2001.[26]

June 9, 2005

Regulation National Market System (NMS) was passed by the SEC on this date. Known as Regulation NMS, this important rule looked to improve the U.S. exchanges through greater fairness in price execution, improve display of quotes, and more access to market data. This new regulation consisted of the Order Protection Rule, which aimed to ensure that investors received the best price when their orders were executed by removing the ability to have orders traded through (executed at a worse price); the Access Rule, which aimed to improve access to quotations from trading centers in the National Market System by requiring greater linking and lower access fees; and the Sub-Penny Rule, which set the quotation increments of all stocks over $1.00 per share to at least $0.01. In addition, Regulation NMS included market data rules that allocated revenue to self-regulatory organizations (SROs) that promoted and improved market data access.[27]

October 14, 2005

On this date, BATS Trading, Inc., received a minority investment from GETCO, LLC. Managing directors Stephen Schuler and Dan Tierney said that "given the opportunity in the rapidly consolidating ECN space, we believe [that] BATS has the right combination of technology, people, and vision to create new levels of innovation and efficiency." Both Schuler and Tierney had a long professional relationship with David Cummings, BATS Trading founder.[28]

June 2, 2006

The NYSE agreed to buy the pan-European Euronext exchange on this date, creating the first transatlantic stock market. The NYSE had edged out its German rival, Deutsche Börse, to clinch the deal, which aimed to create a business worth $20 billion. The new firm would have its U.S. base in New York and international headquarters in Paris and Amsterdam. Little we knew that five years later Deutsche Börse would decide to acquire the combined NYSE Euronext.

Stock exchanges globally were looking to merge as competition for business increased, fueled by the shift into electronic trading. A merged exchange had more appeal because traders, investors, and issuers were all keen to reduce transaction costs, especially in clearing and settlement. For the NYSE, the addition of Paris-based Euronext, which operated bourses in Paris, Amsterdam, Brussels, and Lisbon, was expected to attract businesses that might have been put off by the extensive U.S. regulations implemented after a series of corporate scandals, including the collapse of energy giant Enron.[29]

October 17, 2006

The CME and the Chicago Board of Trade (CBOT), longtime fierce competitors, announced that they would merge in an $8 billion deal on this date, creating the largest market for financial derivatives contracts in the world. The transaction would be the latest in a wave of mergers among the leading financial exchanges as they transform themselves from member-owned clubs to for-profit companies competing in markets that had become increasingly global and electronic.

A combination of the two Chicago markets, which were founded in the nineteenth century to trade agricultural futures, would trumpet the spectacular rise of derivatives, financial contracts whose value is tied to or derived from currencies, interest rates, commodities, or other things of value. Derivatives had made risk more manageable for many businesses, including oil companies seeking to insure themselves against storms and banks trying to protect themselves against home mortgage defaults. Yet they also had fueled trading blow-ups, as in the near collapse in 1998 of the hedge fund Long-Term Capital Management that shook the financial markets. The business of trading such financial contracts had generated huge fortunes that had led many exchanges to begin looking for merger partners. They sought to create greater efficiency and more liquid markets where buyers and sellers more easily found what they wanted for the right price, much as on eBay.[30]

March 30, 2007

On this date, Chi-X Europe was launched by Chi-X Global's parent, Instinet, owned by a consortium of financial institutions and operated independently. Chi-X Europe operated the largest pan-European equity Multilateral Trading Facility (MTF) with a low-cost model designed to help trading participants achieve ultralow execution, clearing, and settlement costs.[31]

What was originally an experiment in the U.S. financial markets quickly turned into an international development, with Instinet's Chi-X Global starting the first European MTF as a prelude to its expansion in Asia. The pace of this evolution was only going to accelerate further.

CHAPTER 2

Meet the Speed Traders: John Netto

"When I was 12, I saw the movie *Wall Street*—the combination of energy on the trading floor, intellectual stimulation, and adrenaline all hooked me. I found my passion, and I knew from that moment forward this was what I wanted to do."

John Netto is the founder and president of M3 Capital. He is the author of *One Shot–One Kill Trading: Precision Trading through the Use of Technical Analysis* (McGraw-Hill, 2004). Netto has worked with buy-side firms, sell-side firms, and technology providers on more efficiently combining structure, strategy, and personnel to increase trading profits. Netto also has published numerous articles and lectured on topics ranging from "Dynamically Delta Hedging Your Option Portfolio," a Eurex white paper entitled, "Techniques and Methodologies for Equity Index Spread Trading," to more qualitative issues such as "The 10 Attributes of a Great Trader." He also has presented on behalf of CME Group, Thomson Reuters, and Golden Networking and makes regular appearances on Forex TV, Fox Business Channel, and many other media outlets.

"I was always encouraged to be entrepreneurial. I had a penchant for risk from a young age and fancied anything with odds, including the markets, sports, and card games. The spark for my career in trading came after watching the movie *Wall Street.* Seeing the vibrancy of the trading floor, the spirit, the energy, the money, and the competition—it stirred a passion in me that was amazing. At that moment, I knew what I needed to do with my future.

"I have always had an interest in the outcome of unpredictable events. From the time I was young, I found an interest in finance and technology, and this continued after I enlisted in the Marine Corps. My parents were active in real estate, so I had an interest in the market when I was a child. Identifying opportunities and finding value was always something that appealed to me.

"I read my first book on derivatives, which accompanied a subscription to the *Wall Street Journal,* when I was 12. It explained the basics of calls and puts, along with other trading vehicles. As a result, I started to learn about options and other related topics, and in high school I continued on that track. Being a Bay Area native, I took the Golden State Economics Exam my senior year in high school. I placed in the top 1 percent for the state, and despite an otherwise poor academic record, I really thought this is something I could do.

"When I got a little older, my motivation became that I wanted to be part of something that continuously stimulated me spiritually, emotionally, and competitively. I also wanted to feel where wealth came from and develop something that created wealth for myself and others. That was success to me. Success to me now means doing what you love and feeling like it isn't work; being able to wake up every day and look forward to doing something. When Monday is your favorite day of the week, you are successful."

The Trader's Path

"My first work experience was in the Marine Corps., which I joined at the age of 18. It was a really worthwhile experience. After being stationed in Japan and working at the U.S. Embassy in Tokyo, I came back to Seattle and attended the University of Washington, majoring in Japanese, Chinese, and Asian studies. During that time, I worked as a business editor there and eventually linked up with a proprietary trading firm in Seattle.

"By 2008, I was a market maker on the former U.S. Futures Exchange (USFE) for the Mini-Dollar DAX contract. Anthony Giacomin, a close colleague of mine, was driving that product, and it really had a chance to become another blockbuster trading vehicle. MF Global owned a material piece of the exchange, so the environment seemed to be right. I had always traded the DAX and a number of other Eurex products, but the real marketability about the Mini-Dollar DAX was the fact that it was denominated in dollars and included the top 30 stocks in Germany.

"It was my job to make a market for this new product, so I had to be aware of different hedging ratios, based on how the euro-denominated DAX was moving over in Frankfurt. So, along with creating hedging models and working, my role as a liquidity provider, the proximity and speed to get information in the model that I created became very time-sensitive. As a result, this was my introduction into a de facto high-frequency network. Advantage Futures, the futures commission merchant (FCM) I cleared through, was a leader in colocation and proximity solutions to a number of futures exchanges, and it was a great first start into true high-frequency trading.

"Because I was arbitraging and balancing my order book based on the equity market out there, I was an alpha tester for CQG's Autospreader, and because CQG was colocated around the world, it was a great way to begin implementing other strategies without the cost constraints faced by so many high-frequency trading firms. I became very active in homogeneous or fungible arbitrage products on futures exchanges. As a result of those initial strategies developed in 2008, M3 Capital has continued developing more strategies and attaching them to more markets, as well as helping other frequency trading managers grow their businesses.

"Based on my experience, my first advice to people who are thinking about a career is to start on their own. Second, if one wants to get a traditional career, what he or she can do now is, given the greater need of people who understand compliance, become familiar with the Dodd-Frank Wall Street Reform and Consumer Protection Act. It would benefit anyone's finance career to read those 2,200 pages of the law and establish a specialty in compliance.

"Compliance is only getting bigger, whereas analyst jobs, for instance, are being compressed as a number of parts of the sell-side brokerage business are being compressed with declining margins. Being in compliance, one can come and work with smaller funds out there, given that those funds can't afford the big compliance firms that many bulge-bracket firms use. It's a great way to get experience and then, in a couple years, get attached to a trading firm. One can work for those small funds as their compliance department because the funds can't afford a full department. In this way, someone who's just starting out can get a job, get some hands-on experience, and get his or her foot in the door."

High-Frequency Trading and Its Impact

John Netto would define *high-frequency trading* as the use of technology to execute a strategy at a velocity that would be unachievable if executed manually.

"A lot of media pundits speak of high-frequency trading in terms way too broad. High-frequency trading in many cases provides greater liquidity and sharper pricing through the use and development of more robust models and a willingness of firms who create those models to take on risk. These models have been spawned as a result of the desire for proprietary trading firms and investors to build more exposure to quantitative strategies."

For Netto, the deadline established by the Securities and Exchange Commission (SEC) in 2001 for all U.S. stock markets to convert to decimals might have been the seminal moment for high-frequency trading.

"It has an intensely data-driven component. Therefore, it is the technology that exists today (or in the last couple of years) that has made the idea of high-frequency trading, or at least setting up automated strategies, much more conducive and much more attainable for a number of firms out there. So, when you look at these various facets and you look at when it all began, it is more of an evolution rather than one watershed date where high-frequency trading formally took off.

"High-frequency trading impacts a lot of different sectors and a lot of different market participants in a lot of different ways. The degree of impact depends on a host of factors, including market conditions, high volatility or low volatility, investors' need for liquidity, and the duration of their holding periods, depending on what you set as spectrum. If one is a short-term scalper and does some things manually, and if one uses a computer, it will be faster and bring opportunities; thus it will definitely have impact. If someone is a trader who wants to take a complex set of strategy criteria and put them into a package so that one can apply this across multiple markets, then high-frequency or, in this case, automated trading will be beneficial because it allows the trader to execute strategies that one previously was not able to do because of lack of infrastructure and technology.

"For the markets, high-frequency trading brings a potentially greater source of liquidity. At the end of the day, this is a positive thing for the economy. Let's take a step back and first look at what the stock market is. The stock market is a place where people look to raise capital to fund and generate further business operations in exchange for giving investors a chance to participate in the company's appreciation. Thus, if the market is more robust and stronger as a result of greater liquidity and sharper pricing, the ability for businesses in America to raise capital and further build the strength of the economy is a positive one. This gives companies the confidence to move forward and can contribute markedly to job growth in this country. If, however, there are questions on the integrity of the markets, whether they are structural in the case of the 'flash crash' on May 6 or ethical as in the case with Enron, then these can have damaging consequences on our ability to continue leading the world in the financial markets. It is a great insurance policy when you have a healthy and robust capital market structure. If high-frequency trading can strengthen the markets to provide another way or another edge of liquidity, it only helps the economy as a whole."

The High-Frequency Trading Controversy

High-frequency traders are famously reluctant to speak to the press for many reasons; first, they wouldn't be interested in disclosing their strategies or providing any indication on how they generate alpha; second, time is money for them because they could be tinkering with their algorithms and launching new strategies; and finally, quite frankly, the most important reason, they are afraid to be misunderstood and misquoted. It was not surprising that the *New York Times* article that uncovered high-frequency trading for mainstream America, "Stock Traders Find Speed Pays, in Milliseconds,"[1] didn't include comments from any high-frequency traders.

"There is a lot of misinformation out there, from some of our leaders in Washington to a lot of finance journalists. Although some really understand high-frequency trading and have done a great job of portraying it to the general public, unfortunately, most of our leaders don't have the sophistication to understand all the nuances. As a result, I hope we do not see legislation based on political whims.

"Since most trading is computer-based, whether it is the Eurex exchange, Globex, the ICE [the InterContinental Exchange (ICE) Trading Platform], or the equity markets, computers and electronic trading have allowed so many people to partake of the market, to manage their portfolios, and to be involved and control their personal wealth. The path to building stronger and more efficient markets inevitably will contain challenges, and this is an inherent part of the evolution. I think the media, which are mandated to explain every event that happens, often misinterpret what is really happening when it comes to high-frequency trading. The paradox is that this can create more trading opportunities as a result."

How a Trader Organizes His Life

"Being that I live in New York City, Las Vegas, and San Francisco, the time zone makes a difference as to how a day plays out.

"In Las Vegas, I typically wake up between 4:30 and 5:00 a.m. I saunter across my house to my trading room and go about the trading day; I work very closely with my brother, and we have all the creature comforts any high-frequency trading firm could ask for. At 1:00 to 1:30 p.m., Pacific time, the U.S. markets have now closed, and after the necessary trade reconciliations have been done, I go to the gym. I think fitness and being active are a very important part of success. Being balanced helps you to keep your core strong and creative.

"There are some stark contrasts between trading in Las Vegas and New York City. Las Vegas brings more of a residential feel to my trading day, as one would expect when a person doesn't have to leave the confines of his home. In New York City, there is more of a shirt and tie, more of a corporate feel. In New York City, I get up at 5:30 a.m., and I go to work out at Equinox right around when it opens; I get back at 7:00 a.m. I normally arrive at the office at around 8:00 a.m. I am there until anywhere from 5:00 to 7:00 p.m. New York City is great, with amazing and talented people. I make it a point to try and meet as many people as possible in and out of the finance industry by going to a lot of networking events and other goings-on. Most days I can't stay up past 10:00 p.m. and promptly pass out at that time so that I can get up and repeat the cycle the next day.

"When I work out of my office in the San Francisco Bay Area, I wake up at 4:30 a.m. and then go in and trade for a couple of hours, depending on what is going on in the market. If something good is going on, I will stay longer. I tend to spend a lot more time on the phone when I am not in New York City in terms of strategy collaboration. When I am in New York or Chicago, it is a lot more hands-on with the traders there.

"I spend many months in different cities, and this typically depends on what is going on with the markets or the money managers I'm working with. For example, I would typically spend the spring and fall in New York City, the summer in San Francisco, and the winter in Las Vegas. It's a lot of traveling, but it suits me well."

Your High-Frequency Trading Operation

"Nowadays, sophisticated investors are actively seeking out managers who employ high-frequency trading strategies. Algorithmic trading strategies have already become widespread, and irrespective of one's definition or perception of what exactly high-frequency trading is, the concept of automation in trading is here to stay because everyone from Goldman Sachs to more retail investors are able to run much more sophisticated strategies."

Netto's company, M3 Capital, has a wide range of alternative investment expertise, contacts, and services to help quantitative-based managers, hedge funds, commodity trading advisors, and professional traders enhance their business model. The company's experience in working with sell-side and buy-side firms, as well as technology service providers, makes it a great conduit for anyone looking for tangible value-add in the alternative investment space. M3 Capital combines the "trinity of trading success" using structure, strategy, and people to help clients generate alpha.[2]

"Running a high-frequency trading operation goes well beyond the strategy. In fact, if you ask most people, the creation of the strategy was the easy part. Issues such as how one will raise capital and how one will handle dealing with compliance, regulatory, reporting, and developing my infrastructure are all questions not asked at first but which become a critical part of the equation of profitability.

"Speaking to the strategy directly, it all depends on what one wants to use it for. Some strategies are developed and run internally, whereas others have appeal because they can be run on super liquid products such as the SPDR S&P 500 [Standard & Poor's Depositary Receipts listed on the NYSE under the ticker symbol SPY] or eMini S&P 500 futures. It's always been my advice to clients and colleagues to piggyback on top of someone else's infrastructure at first as they are getting started so that they can focus on what they do best. From there, you can make an informed decision about how committed you want to become from a capital perspective.

"Low latency, in nearly every case, is very important for high-frequency trading firms, but the degree of importance depends on the strategy and how often it is executed. [As with] visibility of the order flow and institutional orders, it depends on the strategy one is using. In some cases, it is very important; for some others, it is not that important.

"I trade a lot of future markets, equity index futures, commodity futures, fixed-income futures, currency futures, and whatever asset classes fall into those markets. For me, quantitative trading is an important part of my revenues, and I see more opportunities for expansion in the future. Yes, I use capital-efficient products, which contain inherent leverage. I trade options, and I trade the underlying futures products. There are a lot of variables in trading; for example, I use correlation strategies, mean reversion strategies, and trend-following strategies, just to name a few. The hedging techniques depend on how I manage risk behind that strategy and what I am trading.

"I am always looking for better ways to do what I do. It is a natural evolution; as a trader, you can never get complacent, so I am always looking to improve my technology. In terms of infrastructure, I would say buy versus build; if you have a truly special part of the team that can build something that would be the best, go for it. Otherwise, I would say in most cases, from a time standpoint and from the strategy, you are better off buying or leasing.

"I am a little more open-minded when choosing people; I am not looking for the traditional candidate because M3 Capital isn't structured that way. I am more interested in those who have gotten real trading experience or even experience at managing risk, and they know how to take some heat. I also do coventures; someone may come to me, and they may already have a strategy they are developing, and we go into a situation where they may put up some capital and I put up some capital, and we go into that together. What we do is we venture in partnerships with those people where we believe there exists a real opportunity to build value for both sides.

"I want people to have some skin in the game; if someone has a strategy in place, then it is only a matter of time to hit the ground running. So here's how I look at it: If you have all that talent and develop a strategy, let's sit down and talk at that point. People then come to me with something ready to run, and that is how I grow in that way. The compensation comes from being in a goal-congruent deal and being locked side by side. The compensation comes from the collective profits that are made. It comes from the success or failure of the strategy.

"I don't know of a strategy yet, though, that doesn't have losses from time to time, regardless of how well it performs in its theoretical vacuum."

The Future of High-Frequency Trading

"I think high-frequency trading is going to get bigger, stronger, and more prevalent. There are potential regulatory changes that might impact the growth of high-frequency trading; that is always a possibility. They have talked about colocation and proximity legislation, but who knows how it all shakes and if the desired results from this legislation are accomplished.

"I do see more traditional investment managers expanding into high-frequency trading; more managers are using technology as in means of investing. Similarly, more institutional investors are allocating part of their asset base to quantitative trading strategies."

For John Netto, the most sophisticated systems can be thought of as the assistants to the traders, not replacements to the traders, because after all, strategy, structure, and people are the key to success in the market—"that combination of a robust and viable strategy, a market that you can actually execute the strategy in or the structure behind that, and the person who manages or facilitates the overall process or the execution. Automation is to assist the trader but not to replace the trader."

"I think at this moment that the future is more than just technology, which is already very robust; it will be more about adoption of the technology, which will determine how fast things go. Not every exchange has the same technology or robust infrastructure; I think what we will see is that more and more firms, more and more exchanges around the world, will get caught up, and then it will be about the interchangeability of the technology. And not just from a hardware standpoint but also from a software standpoint. Issues such as 'what exchange trade data can we give up to another exchange' and 'how those data get aggregated.' Considering the current environment, the future will be more about data aggregation and data processing and getting those data into the hands of the right people than about who will build the fastest server."

CHAPTER 3

The Path to Growth

By 2007, high-frequency trading was the province of small firms, led by visionaries with prior floor experience who had become sold on the promise of electronic trading, and innovative hedge funds, willing to test the waters. This was about to change, however, because financial players started to take note of the strategies these firms were using to produce consistent profits. For instance, it would later be revealed that while Citadel's biggest funds sustained heavy losses in 2008, Citadel Execution Services, the company's high-frequency operation, flourished, bringing in about $1 billion in profits.

Changes are Coming, 2007–2008

Private equity has always been on the lookout for profit-making opportunities. High-frequency trading couldn't have been the exception, with major firms acquiring stakes in GETCO; RGM Advisors, LLC; and Flow Traders.

April 16, 2007

After two months of speculation, private equity firm General Atlantic, LLC, invested about $300 million in GETCO on this date, in a deal that valued the firm at about $1.5 billion. By then, GETCO was engaged in electronic trading on exchanges, electronic communications networks (ECNs), and alternative trading systems (ATSs) around the world. Bill Ford, CEO, and Rene Kern, managing director, of General Atlantic were joining the GETCO board of directors. There was no change of management or control as a result of this transaction.[1]

May 25, 2007

On this date, the Nasdaq unveiled a takeover of the Nordic stock exchange owner OMX. A merger between OMX, which operated bourses in Sweden, Finland, Denmark, Iceland, and the Baltic states, and the slightly larger Nasdaq would create a £3.5 billion group, leapfrogging the London Stock Exchange (LSE), which is worth £2.7 billion, in terms of market value. An attempt by Nasdaq to merge with the LSE was rejected by LSE investors in January, preventing Nasdaq from making another hostile approach for 12 months. The LSE already had a joint venture with OMX to trade derivatives. Nasdaq had been linked to OMX since the Nordic exchange had confirmed it was in talks with potential partners the prior month. The Swedish government owned a 6.6 percent stake in OMX but was ready to sell this under a privatization program. Investor, the Swedish investment group run by the Wallenberg family, was OMX's biggest investor, with a 10.7 percent shareholding, and was expected to retain its stake.[2]

July 2, 2007

On this date, Citigroup agreed to buy Automated Trading Desk, a closely held company, for $680 million to increase its ability to allow clients worldwide to trade stocks electronically. Founded in 1988, Automated Trading Desk had about 120 broker-dealer customers and traded, on average, more than 200 million shares daily, or 6 percent of the volume on both the NYSE and the Nasdaq.

Citigroup said that it expected the acquisition to double its share of volume on these markets to about 12 percent. It also intended to expand Automated Trading Desk's platform worldwide. Automated Trading Desk would keep its headquarters in Mount Pleasant, South Carolina, and operate as a unit of Citigroup's global equities business.[3]

October 2, 2007

Nasdaq Stock Market, Inc., the second-biggest U.S. equity market, announced plans on this date to buy the Boston Stock Exchange for about $61 million to expand trading and enter the clearing business. The acquisition didn't include the Boston Options Exchange, which had entered talks to sell a majority stake to Montreal Exchange, Inc., owner of Canada's derivatives market.

With its purchase, the Nasdaq would gain a second venue for trading, allowing brokerages to execute transactions more easily by posting quotes on both markets. The acquisition also would give the Nasdaq control of the regulatory arm of the Boston Options Exchange as it prepared to enter the faster-growing business of trading equity derivatives.

Members of the Boston Stock Exchange had approved a plan in February to transform the market into a for-profit company. The Boston Stock Exchange had shuttered its electronic equities market, the Boston Equities Exchange (BeX), created two years before with backing from some of Wall Street's biggest brokerage firms. In acquiring the Boston Stock Exchange, Nasdaq would receive BeX, the Boston Stock Exchange Clearing Corporation, and the Boston Options Exchange Regulation. In addition, Nasdaq would acquire a so-called self-regulatory organization license to trade both stocks and options.[4]

November 1, 2007

On this date, the Markets in Financial Instruments Directive (MiFID) replaced the Investment Services Directive (ISD) as the European Union's instrument providing a harmonized regulatory regime for investment services across the 30 member states of the European Economic Area (the 27 member states of the European Union plus Iceland, Norway, and Liechtenstein). The main objectives of the directive were to increase competition and consumer protection in investment services.

MiFID was the cornerstone of the European Commission's Financial Services Action Plan, whose 42 measures would significantly change how EU financial service markets operate. MiFID was the most significant piece of legislation introduced under the "Lamfalussy procedure," designed to accelerate the adoption of legislation based on a four-level approach recommended by the Committee of Wise Men chaired by Baron Alexandre Lamfalussy. There were three other "Lamfalussy directives"—the Prospectus Directive, the Market Abuse Directive, and the Transparency Directive.

MiFID retained the principles of the EU "passport" introduced by the Investment Services Directive (ISD) but introduced the concept of "maximum harmonization," which placed more emphasis on home-state supervision. This was a change from the prior EU financial service legislation, which had featured a "minimum harmonization and mutual recognition" concept. "Maximum harmonization" didn't permit states to be "superequivalent" or to "gold plate" EU requirements detrimental to a "level playing field." Another change was abolition of the "concentration rule," in which member states could require investment firms to route client orders through regulated markets.

MiFID would require that operators of continuous order-matching systems make aggregated order information on "liquid shares" available at the five best price levels on the buy and sell sides; for quote-driven markets, the best bids and offers of market makers must be made available. MiFID would require firms to publish the price, volume, and time of all trades in listed shares, even if executed outside a regulated market, unless certain requirements were met to allow for deferred publication. Finally, MiFID would require that firms take all reasonable steps to obtain the best possible result in the execution of an order for a client. The "best possible result" would not be limited to execution price but would also include cost, speed, likelihood of execution, likelihood of settlement, and any other factors deemed relevant.[5]

November 30, 2007

On this date, the New York Stock Exchange (NYSE) announced plans to build a 400,000-square-foot data center. The NYSE surprised some industry veterans by deciding to build its own data center. Most exchanges in the past had rented out space to data-center providers. The NYSE had largely kept its facility quiet, even keeping the exact location a closely guarded secret. Executives had made oblique references to the company's plans, describing them as "critical" to the NYSE's future. Certainly, the NYSE was seeking to stem a slide in market share from more than 80 percent in 2004 to about 40 percent in 2009, according to data from Equity Research Desk, a research company in Greenwich, Connecticut.[6]

The NYSE was rolling the dice in hopes that it would become a go-to venue for high-speed trading and was even offering space to other exchanges. The exchange was building a similar facility outside London that would cater to clients who wanted access to overseas markets. The combined price tag for the two data centers would be about $500 million, according to people familiar with the matter. The NYSE had started taking orders for space in the Mahwah, New Jersey facility, internally dubbed "Project Alpha." The exchange expected to attract everyone from large Wall Street banks to traditional brokerages and hedge funds. The NYSE wouldn't say how many customers had signed up.

January 28, 2008

On this date, private equity and buyout firm TA Associates announced that it had completed a minority equity investment in RGM Advisors, LLC, an automated trading firm. Kenneth Schiciano and Kurt Jaggers, managing directors at TA Associates, would be joining the board of directors of RGM. Just the year before, General Atlantic, LLC, had invested in competitor GETCO. Both firms were not exactly looking for trading capital but for equity; knowing that no sane high-frequency trader would like his or her firm to go through an initial public offering (IPO), private equity seemed to provide the best of both worlds: access to capital and private ownership.

Founded in 2001, RGM had applied scientific methods and computing power to trade in multiple asset classes around the world using high-frequency automated strategies. The company's team of professionals included software developers, information technologists, engineers, and scientists with backgrounds in computer science, physics, chemistry, ecology, and mathematics. RGM was based in Austin, Texas, and maintained a London office.[7]

June 5, 2008

On this date, Flow Traders, one of Europe's leading electronic trading firms, announced that it had received a minority equity investment from Summit Partners, a private equity and venture capital firm. Flow Traders, founded in 2004 and headquartered in Amsterdam, the Netherlands, was an electronic market making business focused on high-growth asset classes. Flow Traders traded equities as well as derivatives, currencies, and bonds in the main European markets. The company operated from offices in Amsterdam and Singapore and traded on more than 25 electronic exchanges and trading venues.[8]

By raising private-equity capital, GETCO, TA Associates, and Flow Traders were able to strengthen their equity standing and provide a payoff to their founders and stakeholders, all through cashing in at the best times. This would have been impossible to pull off just a few months later.

Extraordinary Market Conditions, 2008

The most difficult time for the most established financial players brought a different tune to the high-frequency trading industry. While Lehman Brothers was collapsing, Renaissance's Medallion would go on to gain 80 percent by the end of the year, thanks in part to its focus on taking advantage of short-term swings, both up and down, in all kinds of markets.

July 17, 2008

On this date, Goldman Sachs' Sigma X dark pool executed 406 million shares, making it the seventh-largest market center for U.S. equities. Sigma X's volume was up 100 percent over the previous seven weeks, according to Rishi Nangalia, head of product development at Goldman Sachs Electronic Trading. "It's a virtuous circle," he had said. "We have more volume passing through from more clients and their algorithms, and as a result of higher fill rates, we get more flow, which in turn further increases the match rates."[9] This surge was taking place against a backdrop of higher equity-market volume overall and greater volatility.

Goldman wasn't the only broker dark pool breaking records. Credit Suisse on Wednesday logged an all-time high of 210 million shares in CrossFinder, its dark-liquidity pool. Executed volume in the pool grew an average of 30 percent per month in 2008, according to the broker. Dan Mathisson, head of Credit Suisse's Advanced Execution Services group, had noted that his firm and Goldman had "separated from the pack" of several dozen dark pools. "We're hitting that fun part of a crossing platform, the liquidity-begets-liquidity phase," he said.

One reason for the jump, according to Mathisson, was the "network effect" of institutions increasingly accessing dark liquidity through algorithms. Smart order routing and heat-map-type technology that routed orders to "hot" destinations providing fills "lead to a disproportionate increase in the market share of the bigger pools," he said. "Flow is migrating off traditional destinations to destinations that barely existed a couple of years ago."[10]

Goldman Sachs, Credit Suisse, and a couple of other brokers had seen their volumes race past Liquidnet's. However, unlike these broker internalization pools, Liquidet and competitors Pipeline and ITG's BLOCKalert, and to a lesser extent, ITG's POSIT were block pools that attracted institutional flow before it got broken up and sent into the market in pieces.[11]

September 8, 2008

UAL Corp. shares fell 76 percent to $3 after a nearly six-year-old *Chicago Tribune* news story on the 2002 bankruptcy filing of the firm was posted on the Bloomberg financial news service on this date. "The magnitude of the decline might underscore the lack of confidence investors had in UAL and the troubled airline industry in general. UAL Corp., parent of United Airlines, and several news organizations involved were blindsided by the resurrection of the *Chicago Tribune* article. UAL Corp., which exited bankruptcy more than two years [previously], demanded a retraction by the *Florida*

Sun-Sentinel, where the out-of-date report first appeared. Trade in UAL Corp. shares was halted on the Nasdaq after the old report hammered shares. The stock rebounded somewhat when trading resumed, ending down 11.2 percent at $10.92, compared with the Amex airline index .XAL, which fell 2.3 percent."[12]

According to Adam Lei and Huihua Li, the share volume and the number of trades were significantly higher during the event window (23.03 million shares and 70,520 trades, respectively) than during the nonevent periods (0.72 million shares and 2,465 trades, respectively). For them, the 70,520 trades during the 10-minute event window translate into 117.53 trades per second—an indication of high-frequency trading.[13]

October 15, 2008

On this date, Kenneth Griffin, head of Citadel Investment Group, one of the world's most successful and influential hedge funds, sent a letter to investors after rumors about its performance helped drag down the stock market. September, he wrote, was the "single worst month, by far, in the history of Citadel. Our performance reflected extraordinary market conditions that I did not fully anticipate, combined with regulatory changes driven more by populism than policy."

For 2006 and 2007, Citadel's main funds, Kensington and Wellington, had returned about 30 percent annually. Griffin had written in his letter that 2007 "was the most successful year in the history of our firm." Its core strategy had long been convertible-bond arbitrage, which allowed investors to profit from differences in the movements of convertible bonds and other securities. In the summer of 2008, Citadel had increased investments in that area. "Regretfully, I did not foresee the financial disaster that was to unfold in September," he wrote in the letter.

The financial crisis dramatically raised the cost of borrowing and reduced the availability of credit, he wrote, reducing the value of cash assets compared with the value of derivative instruments. At the same time, the decision of regulators around the world to temporarily ban the short selling of equities "created material dislocations across many of our portfolios and disrupted our ability to assume and manage risk."[14]

Not surprisingly, Tactical Trading, a small internal team led by Misha Malyshev, was seeing returns significantly higher that the hedge funds. After several months of development, the group had its first profitable day using high-frequency trading on July 25, 2004. Since then, Tactical Trading had been nothing but positive, earning about $75 million in returns the following year, nearly $500 million in 2006, and $892 million in 2007, when Tactical Trading was spun out from Citadel's flagship hedge funds. This turned out to be a bad move for the Kensington and Wellington funds, which plummeted along with much of the rest of the hedge fund industry in 2008.[15] But the Tactical Trading fund, which managed about $1.9 billion employing high-frequency strategies, saw earnings of $1.15 billion, operating with just around 55 people.[16]

October 24, 2008

On this date, BATS Holdings announced its much-anticipated launch of BATS Exchange, one of the fastest-growing top-tier equity markets in the United States. BATS launched with two active symbols, Aeropostale, Inc. (ARO), and Arena Pharmaceuticals, Inc. (ARNA), and would be active in all U.S. symbols as of Thursday, November 6. BATS, which had filed for exchange status in November 2007 and received approval in August 2008, matched about 12 percent of daily U.S. equity volume.[17]

October 31, 2008

On this date, BATS Europe, the multilateral trading facility (MTF) owned by U.S. exchange group BATS Trading, started trading 10 U.K.-listed securities, roughly one year after the European MiFID had gone live. As with other MTFs, BATS Europe employed a maker-taker pricing model. It had matched Chi-X's pricing, charging 0.3 basis point for taking liquidity and paying a 0.2-basis-point rebate for posting liquidity. This made BATS Europe cheaper than Turquoise but more expensive than Nasdaq OMX Europe, which had recently adjusted both its fee and rebate to 0.25 basis point as part of a pricing promotion, effectively making trading on the platform free.

BATS Europe would embark on a phased launch, culminating in full trading of all LSE-, Euronext-, and Xetra-traded stocks on November 19.

BATS' arrival in Europe had been hotly anticipated. Its U.S. incarnation had succeeded in grabbing significant market share when it launched as an ECN in January 2006, despite being one of the later ECNs to set up. The platform had a U.S. market share of 12 percent[18] despite its humble beginnings. BATS had started from scratch and built a financial vehicle designed for speed. Speed had been essential because the target audience for BATS wasn't retail investors but the types of hedge funds that executed thousands of trades per day—high-frequency trading. And for such funds, which sought to capture microscopic gains, speed really mattered. As a result, when BATS went live in January 2006, most of the advanced trading platforms could execute a trade in 1 to 30 milliseconds; BATS started with a speed of 1 to 3 milliseconds. Equally important, BATS had been able to offer highly favorable economic terms to traders who used the system because it operated in a lower-cost environment (Kansas City) than its big-city competitors.[19] At some moment, about 60 percent of BATS' volume was coming from automated market makers or high-frequency trading firms.

Volume and Volatility in 2009

Drivers for the enormous returns of Renaissance's Medallion, Citadel's Tactical Trading, and other high-frequency trading firms in 2008 were volume, thanks to the exponential growth of electronic trading, and volatility, something that was not missed in the second half of the year. Not willing to miss the business of the ever-growing number of high-frequency trading firms, Direct Edge, the Nasdaq, and BATS started offering their versions of "flash orders." The incendiary combination of a terrific 2008 and the availability of flash orders ultimately would lead to a *New York Times* article uncovering the industry and blowing its efforts to stay under the radar.

January 26, 2009

"For firms like us that are short-term- and technology-focused, the big drivers are volume and volatility," said Nathan Laurell, director of market making and an owner of Infinium Capital Management, which had hired 60 of its 210 employees in 2008 and was still adding staff. Hiring at the trading firms, which employed thousands, had helped to offset some of the layoffs sweeping the city's financial sector. And their surging profits showed that a certain Chicago-style trading strategy dating to the earliest days of the futures exchanges was as viable as ever.[20]

February 19, 2009

Misha Malyshev, who had headed Citadel's high-frequency trading team, resigned from the firm, *Bloomberg News* reported on this date. Two members of the 60-strong high-frequency team had left with him. Citadel's high-frequency group traded for two of its hedge funds, both of which returned about 40 percent in 2008 amid an otherwise awful year for the firm. Its flagships, the Kensington and Wellington funds, lost more than half their value.

Owing to his employment contract with Citadel, Malyshev would have been expected to take time off before joining a new firm or starting his own fund within the next 18 months, Bloomberg reported.[21] Ultimately, Malyshev would start Teza Technologies, LLC, and get sued by Citadel.

March 2, 2009

Goldman Sachs Electronic Trading expanded its global crossing capabilities with the launch of SIGMA X in Hong Kong on this date. "The growth potential of Hong Kong's market remains significant, and we think alternative pools of liquidity will play an important role in this development going forward," Gene Reilly, managing director and head of trading and execution for Goldman Sachs in Asia, said in a company news release.

Goldman Sachs' SIGMA X was composed of a host of liquidity participants, including hedge funds, institutions, and broker-dealers, as well as flow from Goldman Sachs' trading desks. SIGMA X was the largest nondisplayed liquidity pool in the United States based on equity shares traded daily, according to the release.

SIGMA X Hong Kong was a fully licensed ATS and would allow trading for stocks listed on the Hong Kong Stock Exchange, the release noted. "Our global experiences in alternative liquidity pools, our diverse range of clients, and our continued focus on maintaining a high-quality pool of nondisplayed liquidity means that SIGMA X will deliver substantial value to customers," said Shuya Kekke, managing director and head of Asian GSET, in the release.[22]

June 1, 2009

On this date, Nasdaq Stock Market, Inc., launched two types of "flash" orders that would give participants a chance to fill an order by disseminating it to market participants before it is routed to the public markets. Nasdaq's Routable Flash Order would check its own order book first, and if the order was not filled, it would go ahead and flash that order to its participants via Nasdaq's proprietary ITCH feed.

"This order will basically flash out to our ITCH participants, who are both customers and noncustomers, and it will flash to them for up to 500 milliseconds," explained Brian Hyndman, senior vice president of Nasdaq Transaction Services. Nasdaq was offering a second order type, called the INET-Only Flash, which exposed the order to participants for execution without routing out to the public markets. "This will give customers the ability to get very aggressive and flash an order out to our ITCH participants or (market data) vendors and stay there for up to 500 milliseconds. If there is no execution, it will most likely cancel back to them," according to Hyndman.

The topic of flash orders was sparking considerable debate in the industry over whether holding these orders for fractions of a second and showing them to a large class of market participants and market data vendors was fair to investors. In a letter filed with the Securities and Exchange Commission (SEC), NYSE Euronext, operator of the New York Stock Exchange (NYSE), had opposed the practice and asked the regulator to intervene in Nasdaq's and BATS' plans.[23]

June 4, 2009

Following on the Nasdaq's announcement to introduce flash orders, BATS Exchange introduced BATS Optional Liquidity Technology (BOLT) on this date. Marketable BATS-Only BOLT orders were displayed to market participants for up to 500 milliseconds before being canceled, whereas routable BOLT orders were exposed to participants for up to 25 milliseconds before they were canceled or routed to other market centers.

Order types that briefly display unfilled marketable orders to a trading venue's members before routing them elsewhere could benefit the buy side, but there also were potential dangers inherent in their use, industry experts suggested. The practice of using so-called flash order types first came to prominence in early 2006 when U.S. equities trading platform Direct Edge launched its Enhanced Liquidity Provider (ELP) program. Under this scheme, if an order couldn't be matched on Direct Edge, an indication of interest (IOI) would be sent to the participating liquidity providers, typically brokers and high-frequency proprietary traders. If there was still no match, the order would be routed on or canceled based on the user's instructions.[24]

July 3, 2009

On this date, Sergey Aleynikov, a Goldman Sachs Group, Inc., computer programmer who had quit the prior month, was arrested by FBI agents as he got off a plane at Newark Liberty International Airport. According to a complaint, Aleynikov had downloaded 32 megabytes of data from Goldman's computer system with "the intent to convert that trade secret to the economic benefit of someone other than the owner." Aleynikov worked on programs that were used primarily by Goldman's principal traders, who took risks with the New York company's capital because they bought securities from clients that might end up on Goldman's balance sheet.

According to the FBI, Aleynikov had received a job offer earlier at Chicago's Teza Technologies, LLC, which planned to triple the $400,000-a-year salary he was paid at Goldman. At Goldman, Aleynikov had signed a standard confidentiality pact requiring him to handle all nonpublic information "in strict confidence." The agreement also required that any nonpublic documents that he obtained while working at Goldman would be returned on his departure.[25]

July 9, 2009

On this date, Citadel Investment Group, LLC, the $12 billion hedge fund firm founded by Ken Griffin, sued three former executives and the firm they started, Teza Technologies, LLC, over claims that they violated noncompetition agreements. The firm sought a court order barring the individual defendants from conducting any business through Teza or related entities that compete with Citadel for the duration of the agreements.

Teza had described itself in a July 6 e-mail as a "formative" firm that was neither trading nor investing. Named after a river in western Russia, the Chicago-based firm had been founded by Misha Malyshev, Jace Kohlmeier, and Matt Hinerfeld. All were named as defendants in the complaint. Malyshev had worked at Citadel for almost six years and, until February, was its head of high-frequency trading. He had been on the team that ran a $1.8 billion tactical trading fund that used computer models to make trades every few seconds. That fund had climbed 40 percent in 2008, whereas Citadel's main funds had tumbled 55 percent. Kohlmeier worked under Malyshev at Citadel, and Hinerfeld was an in-house attorney who helped the firm draft employment agreements.[26]

July 21, 2009

Citadel Investment Group, LLC, announced on this date that it was taking a "majority stake" in Equiduct Trading, a European alternative trading system seeking to wrest business from established exchanges, Equiduct's CEO, Artur Fischer, said. Equiduct, operated by the Berlin bourse, was competing with Chi-X Europe, which started in March 2007 and was the first MTF to challenge traditional exchanges, including Deutsche Börse AG, London Stock Exchange Group PLC, and NYSE Euronext, by offering lower fees and faster trading times. Chi-X Europe, which had received a minority investment from GETCO, was the second-largest market by share of trading for stocks listed on all three bourses.[27] Unbeknownst to market participants, Peter Randall, former Chi-X Europe's CEO who had retired just a few months earlier, would later accept the same post at Equiduct Trading, intensifying the competition among European MTFs.

Despite the tremendous growth of the industry (New York and Chicago had seen an explosion in the number of firms) and uniquely positive results under the most adverse conditions, high-frequency trading had managed to stay under the radar. This was about to change on the morning of July 23.

CHAPTER 4

Meet the Speed Traders: Aaron Lebovitz

"Success for me is just about excellence; it is doing whatever I am doing at the moment as well as I can do it."

Throughout his almost two decades in the industry, Aaron Lebovitz has acquired a strong knowledge of mathematical finance with experience implementing risk-neutral approaches to price options, as well as structural and fundamental economic models for pricing various derivatives across most asset classes. In a few years, Lebovitz built the algorithmic and event-driven trading department at Infinium Capital Management, a proprietary capital management firm with offices in Chicago and New York, into an exceptional force in the industry.

Infinium was founded in Chicago in 2001 and built by a core team with decades of experience in trading, software development, and financial modeling. As with most high-frequency trading firms, Infinium has no outside investors and only manages its own money. The company has a long history of partnering with exchanges to launch new products, increase participation in existing products, and solve technology issues. Infinium's culture draws on the experiences of its founders and the business lessons learned through a variety of successful startups and career paths. Infinium's people are extremely intelligent and extraordinarily driven; they are ambitious innovators who constantly seek new opportunities for growth.

Education and First Opportunities

"I grew up in Glencoe, Illinois, in the Chicago area. I was in accelerated math programs as early as second grade, and spent parts of junior high and high school commuting at night to various places for advanced-math instruction. I got my first computer in 1983—an Apple II. I learned to program in Basic in 1979 on a Commodore PET they had at my grade school. I first became interested in finance when I read my father's subscription to *Technical Analysis of Stocks and Commodities* [a Seattle-based monthly magazine about commodity futures contracts, stocks, options, derivatives, and Forex, established in 1982] while I was in high school.

"I received my undergraduate degree in mathematics from Columbia University, New York City, where I also minored in geology, in 1992. After spending the first five years of my career at large banks in New York City, I returned to my hometown of Chicago, where I completed a Ph.D. in finance from the Graduate School of Business at the University of Chicago in 2002. My advice for any current college and graduate students considering a career in finance and high-frequency trading is to be humble, hook up with a firm that has a proven track record, and make sure to know how to write code.

"My first professional opportunity was at Andersen Consulting in 1992; I only lasted eight months before I jumped ship and got into quantitative fixed-income research. My first trading job began in 1995 when I moved from Prudential Securities to Chemical Bank, where some former colleagues at Prudential Securities had moved the year before to build a structured products group. I loved the pace and the competition of trading, and I especially liked the integration of formal models into our trading decisions."

Lebovitz's typical day is spent either working or enjoying time with his family. His hobbies mostly revolve around his three children (ages 10, 8, and 2) because he wants to share time with them. Right now, that is soccer, but they have recently gone through phases of improvisational comedy, LEGO building, and playing video games (such as Xbox or Wii). He and the family love traveling and try to go to at least two new places every year.

The Essence of High-Frequency Trading

"I got into high-frequency trading during my Ph.D. studies, when I consulted for a couple of asset managers in Chicago, and I saw that there was an opportunity to integrate my knowledge of coding, rigorous mathematical modeling, and trading in an emerging field. My first high-frequency strategy was a U.S. equity pairs trading strategy.

"High-frequency trading is typically defined by the number of times a strategy trades during a particular time period, say, 25 trades per day. I think it has evolved in the popular vernacular to narrowly include only strategies where low-latency technology provides some edge. That being said, the most profitable high-frequency trading strategies change by the month.

"The mission statement for algorithmic trading at Infinium is 'Developing new markets, increasing global market liquidity, and driving efficient price discovery.' We live this daily, and I believe we accomplish it. I also believe that most high-frequency traders do the same and that this is to the overall benefit of the market, primarily by reducing the cost and increasing the immediacy of risk transfer. The best analogy here is to the rise of Internet retailers: consumers ('retail') benefited immediately from increased transparency; they could find price information from many vendors all in one place and quickly.

"High-frequency trading has had a similar effect for retail investors; they are able to find better prices and tighter markets and experiment faster execution with more detail on how their execution lines up to public markets than ever before. Summarizing, high-frequency trading brings increased efficiency, which reduces transaction costs. High-frequency trading is able to use automation to produce liquidity more cheaply than in the past and to ensure that information is reflected in prices more quickly than ever before."

The Cultural Perception of High-Frequency Trading

Perception could have become reality if May 6 had not happened and high-frequency traders had not been forced to leave their computers and face CNBC. Lebovitz admits that the industry historically has been secretive about its activities for various reasons. Some of this has to do with safeguarding intellectual property, but it also has to do with the creative destruction that this technological revolution has catalyzed. Some very established, very powerful industry players saw high-frequency trading as a threat to their distribution channels or to their trading desks' ability to get paid for providing liquidity. That created a disincentive for high-frequency traders to advertise their presence. Says Lebovitz: "It had become quite clear that there was a lack of information out there regarding the activities and contributions of high-frequency traders, which has, in turn, led to some misinformation filling the gaps. As practitioners, we have a responsibility to change that."

Lebovitz considers the biggest misconception about the industry to be that high-frequency trading is somehow a new kind of trading. For him, most of high-frequency trading is just automating the routine tasks that traders have been performing for decades. The second-biggest misconception is that high-frequency trading is about making money at the expense of end users. In fact, Lebovitz says, high-frequency trading is about innovating with technology to reduce market frictions: "When Wal-Mart figured out how to use technology to improve logistics and reduce costs, who benefited? The consumer. Who didn't benefit? Sears, Kmart, the other stores that were trying do the same thing but with a higher cost structure. The analogy is not perfect, but you get the point."

For Lebovitz, the biggest risk associated with the growth of high-frequency trading is the same risk the trading industry has always faced. In their rush to get into a new space such as high-frequency trading, some firms can get sloppy and therefore fail to understand and prepare for the consequences of their algorithms potentially going awry. "The great thing in this case is that we are getting out in front of things before that happens," observes Lebovitz. "Some of the smartest guys in the industry and in Washington are all over these issues, and while some off-the-wall ideas have been floated, we are circling in on developing industry best practices and regulatory controls that will minimize both the risk of problems occurring and the impact of any problems that do occur. The biggest danger right now is that we create a regulatory environment that puts too much of a chill on legitimate trading activity and drives up costs of trading for retail and institutional investors."

23.5 Hours a Day, 6 Days a Week

Infinium trades and makes markets electronically, on exchange floors and over the counter (OTC), 23.5 hours a day, 6 days a week. The company seeks to maximize returns and minimize losses by trading a variety of uncorrelated strategies, adhering to stringent money-management rules, and using exceptional people and software. Infinium's market makers use cutting-edge technology and financial modeling to provide liquidity while avoiding unreasonable risk.

The algorithmic strategies that Lebovitz and his people use trade momentary pricing anomalies in the global marketplace. Infinium's advanced communication systems allow traders to see market changes as they occur, whereas its sophisticated software can adapt almost instantaneously to incorporate—and profit from—these changes. Infinium is active on the Chicago Mercantile Exchange, Chicago Board Options Exchange, Intercontinental Exchange, New York Stock Exchange (NYSE)/LIFFE (originally the acronym for the London International Financial Futures Exchange)/Arca, Dubai Gold and Commodities Exchange, Dubai Mercantile Exchange, Eurex, and foreign exchange and fixed-income electronic communications networks (ECNs) across the following asset classes: equity indices, fixed income, energies, foreign exchange, precious metals, and commodities and softs.

"We started back in 2003. We really just had a dozen or so PCs and a really good software platform that took about a year to build. The software available from vendors is now quite powerful, but it is not a fair comparison because the market has matured quite a bit.

"It is safe to say that someone is making money in any given market conditions, but I think there are very few traders, high-frequency or otherwise, making money in all market conditions. It is funny indeed that the question of how high-frequency traders can achieve consistent profits irrespective of market conditions easily could be applied to dealer desks, pit locals, or any other type of trader. And the answer is: if you can adapt your trading approach to changing market conditions, you will be consistently profitable. If you can't, you won't be. In our case, we do use leverage; much of what we trade is leveraged by construction (e.g., options and futures); that being said, we have losses all the time, occasionally significant.

"The importance of low latency and colocation depends on the firm. For very simple trades, where there is competition among firms to provide the same service (e.g., making markets or effecting price discovery), there can be 'races' where low latency is critical. In other cases, where firms have developed complex or subtle strategies, it becomes less of a race, and latency is less important. This is really a key to future success in high-frequency trading, closer to traditional alpha generation than to providing liquidity or enforcing arbitrage relationships.

"Visibility of the order flow and institutional orders is another topic that applies generically to trading—dealer desks, pit locals, and high-frequency traders all want to understand where the market is at any given time, and understanding flows is important to minimize risk and avoid adverse selection. The irony here is that high-frequency firms are actually at a direct disadvantage to banks, for example, in foreign exchange markets, where banks spend large amounts of time and money reverse engineering their customers' trades to attempt to exclude firms that trade profitably with them.

"Buying is cheaper, can be faster to market, and tends to be more general in its applicability. Building in-house is more expensive; there is more risk because you could end up with software inferior to vendor solutions. The upside to building is that if you do it well, you can build customized solutions that are better for specific problems than any 'bought' solution."

Infinium was one of the few firms that didn't turn off its machines on May 6, 2010. According to Lebovitz, his firm traded uninterrupted in most markets throughout the entire day. "None of our trades were canceled. I'm quite comfortable saying that our activity did nothing to accelerate or exacerbate the volatility that day.

"In this regard, I think the 'Preliminary Findings Regarding the Market Events of May 6, 2010' report prepared jointly by the staffs of the CFTC [Commodity Futures Trading Commission] and SEC [Securities and Exchange Commission] has a good analysis of what happened that day. What I think it missed was that the liquidity trap that day was closely tied to global economic conditions, there was tremendous fear about the state of European banks, and even the stability of some governments, and risk appetites diminished significantly in the days leading up to May 6, 2010."

The Future of High-Frequency Trading

"The future of high-frequency trading is still very much in doubt, hinging on an uncertain regulatory environment. High level, there likely will be some consolidation of midsized high-frequency firms. Since the activities of high-frequency traders are not significantly different from the historical role of dealers and locals, this is really just about the maturing of technological innovations in a traditional industry. Technology trends that can be seen on the horizon of high-frequency trading include falling costs, converging technologies, and more standardization and accessibility (through aggregated providers).

"I definitely see more traditional investment managers expanding into high-frequency trading, certainly to improve their execution, probably through partners or executing brokers. That being said, I don't foresee more traditional investment managers shifting their focus to becoming market makers or developing statistical arbitrage strategies.

"I believe that some sophisticated retail investors also will be able to run high-frequency trading strategies. Costs continue to fall rapidly, brokers are increasingly providing customizable services, and technology is maturing to the point that gaps in performance have narrowed by several orders of magnitude since as recently as five years ago. All that said, this is a tough, competitive industry; I would not recommend that anyone who is not willing to focus on it full time risk much of their own money, whether it is in high-frequency trading, commodities speculation, or fundamental value investing.

"In terms of the future, the biggest regulatory concern regarding high-frequency trading is how the rules on so-called disruptive trading practices will be defined and enforced. I think the existing rules on antimanipulation are sufficient for enforcement, and the regulatory agencies could focus more on understanding good and bad high-frequency practices and then enforcing existing rules rather than trying to draft static rules for specific practices."

CHAPTER 5

High-Frequency Trading Goes Mainstream

Only a few weeks after both the Nasdaq and BATS started offering "flash order" functionality to their customers, the *New York Times* ran a piece that completely altered the high-frequency trading landscape.

Stock Traders Find That Speed Pays

It was almost the end of the week, Friday, July 24, 2009, when high-frequency traders learned that they had found a way to master the stock market, peek at investors' orders, and, critics said, even subtly manipulate share prices. "It is called *high-frequency trading*—and it is suddenly one of the most talked-about and mysterious forces in the markets," proclaimed the *New York Times*' Charles Duhigg when he presented high-frequency trading to the general public. "Powerful computers, some housed right next to the machines that drive marketplaces like the New York Stock Exchange, enable high-frequency traders to transmit millions of orders at lightning speed and, their detractors contend, reap billions at everyone else's expense. These systems are so fast they can outsmart or outrun other investors, humans and computers alike. And after growing in the shadows for years, they are generating lots of talk."

It was an interesting turn of events; before a former Goldman Sachs programmer was accused earlier that month of stealing secret computer codes, not many people had heard about high-frequency trading. The article quoted William H. Donaldson, former chairman and chief executive of the New York Stock Exchange (NYSE) and today an advisor to a big hedge fund: "This is where all the money is getting made; if an individual investor doesn't have the means to keep up, they're at a huge disadvantage."

Duhigg's article saw no benefit from high-frequency trading, and that was the impression readers were left with: "High-frequency traders often confound other investors by issuing and then canceling orders almost simultaneously. Loopholes in market rules give high-speed investors an early glance at how others are trading. And their computers can essentially bully slower investors into giving up profits—and then disappear before anyone even knows they were there."[1]

As was expected, immediately after the *New York Times* article was published, Senator Charles Schumer (D., N.Y.) told the Securities and Exchange Commission (SEC) in a letter that he would move to limit flash orders if the agency didn't. SEC chairman Mary L. Schapiro responded by promising to curb any "inequity" in such orders as part of the agency's review of high-speed trading practices. At issue were order types that routed trades through private liquidity pools before being sent onto other exchanges for filling. Those with access to the so-called flash orders, which were made and taken away simultaneously, could see how the market reacted to a flashed order and then place equities bets accordingly. Several people close to SEC discussions on the matter said that the securities regulator was moving to crack down on such order types even before Senator Schumer's letter.[2]

Critics, said the note, had argued that having private-quote data available to some investors—those with access to the private liquidity pools—and not to all created a two-tiered system of investors where those with access could get a better price than those without. While anyone could gain access to flash orders for a fee, only very powerful computers were able to process and act on the information. Getting flashed an order offered traders a distinctive edge. When buy and sell orders come into an exchange, they're first flashed to those paying to see them for 0.03 seconds before they are made available to everyone else. Almost instantly, the systems could detect patterns and get a jump on other investors.[3]

Only a few weeks later, on August 3, 2009, the Financial Services Authority (FSA), Britain's financial regulator, announced that it was examining the impact of high-frequency trading, following up on the SEC steps. The FSA was in talks with some investment banks, hedge funds, and asset managers to assess how high-frequency trading was affecting equity markets. The talks were at an early stage and didn't constitute a formal inquiry. The agency also was assessing the British equity market, including exchanges, dark pools, alternative trading facilities, and other market changes that arose after a European Union rule that took effect in 2007.[4]

Even before that, though, on September 1, 2009, BATS Exchange and Nasdaq OMX Group had stopped offering so-called flash orders to their clients. It was a concerted move aimed at influencing Direct Edge, the company that had pioneered the practice and continued to offer flash orders. These orders accounted for about 25 percent of Direct Edge's profit, even though they represented only 5 percent of its trading volume.

According to the *Wall Street Journal*, "the flash strategy takes a stock order, after it has been checked against a market's main order book, and 'flashes' it to a select group of participants, who have a fraction of a second to act on the order before it is routed to other exchanges to be filled. The practice has helped exchanges build market share but has come under fire from critics who allege [that] it gives some participants an unfair advantage. Flash orders found themselves in the spotlight earlier in 2009, with some claiming they give unfair advantage to some groups of investors at the expense of others."[5]

Finally, on September 17, 2009, the SEC proposed banning flash orders. Mary L. Schapiro, chairwoman of the SEC, had said that in proposing the ban, the commission was attempting to balance the often competing interests of long-term investors and short-term traders because the practice may create a two-tiered market. This would result from allowing only selected participants to access information about the best-available prices for listed securities.[6]

How the Nasdaq and NYSE Euronext Responded to the BATS Challenge

Direct Edge and BATS were eating the Nasdaq's and NYSE Euronext's lunch. BATS had traded 10.6 percent of exchange-listed securities in February 2010 compared with Direct Edge's 9.6 percent, according to data in a Barclays report dated March 1. NYSE Euronext, which operated three platforms, including the NYSE, was the largest U.S. marketplace, with 27.6 percent of volume, followed by Nasdaq OMX Group, Inc., which operated two venues for equities trading and accounted for 24.5 percent.

In order to recover lost terrain, Nasdaq OMX Group, Inc., had announced in late 2009 the rollout of new enhancements and upgrades to its core trading technology known as INET, the common technology used across Nasdaq OMX's U.S. and European markets that also served as the backbone for Genium, Nasdaq OMX's commercial exchange technology offering. Nasdaq OMX technology had a global footprint, supporting the operations of over 70 exchanges, clearing organizations, and central securities depositories in more than 50 countries.[7]

Both exchanges also saw a threat coming from data center operators offering colocation services to more and more high-frequency trading firms. On April 23, 2010, NYSE Euronext asked U.S. regulators to boost oversight of the data centers providing services to brokers and high-frequency traders to ensure that the companies operated fairly. NYSE, which was building two data centers outside New York and London, said in a letter published on the SEC's Web site that rival offerings from Savvis, Inc., Equinix, Inc., and Telx Group, Inc., should be forced to operate as facilities of regulated exchanges to prevent a "tilted playing field." The access they provide to the main computers of exchanges, called *colocation*, allowed firms to transact orders faster. "Not all markets are regulated equally, which creates competitive disadvantages among marketplaces offering colocation," NYSE Euronext told the SEC. That "creates an opportunity for market participants to engage in regulatory arbitrage" and presents a situation in which independent data centers are "under no obligation to ensure fair access" to services.

Responding to the NYSE Euronext assertion, Equinix, a provider of colocation and connection services between 18 markets in the United States, Europe, and Asia, told the SEC that data centers shouldn't be controlled by exchanges. Independent data centers lower costs for customers by enabling them to connect through multiple network providers and to choose which products they want, the Foster City, California–based firm said in a letter to the commission.[8]

In a similar move, ICAP, PLC, said on January 12, 2010, that it had started an algorithmic trading platform as the world's largest broker of trades between banks, seeking to woo investors who execute thousands of transactions using mathematical algorithms to exploit small price moves. ICAP ALX, which would offer a "range" of trading algorithms, had been developed with Arctic Lake Systems, the company said in an e-mailed statement. The system would be offered to ICAP Equities' clients in the first quarter of 2010, the firm said.

London-based ICAP was building an equities business with more than 200 employees in eight countries. In 2009, the company also opened BlockCross, an alternative trading system and so-called dark pool for stocks. European exchanges and brokers began introducing algorithmic trading products as demand boomed in Europe.[9]

Chi-X Europe, the Trailblazer Across the Pond

While the United States saw the emergence of Direct Edge and BATS as operators of alternative trading systems (ATSs), Europe had Chi-X Europe, the first so-called multilateral trading facility (MTF) to challenge traditional bourses, including Deutsche Börse AG, London Stock Exchange Group, PLC, and NYSE Euronext. Launched in March 2007 with backing from Merrill Lynch & Co., Citigroup, Inc., UBS AG, Credit Suisse Group AG, and Morgan Stanley, 7 months ahead of the Markets in Financial Instruments Directive (MiFID) and 18 months ahead of other MTFs, Chi-X Europe offered trading in more than 1,300 of the most liquid securities across 24 indices in 15 European markets, in addition to exchange-traded funds (ETFs), exchange-traded commodities (ETCs), and international depositary receipts (IDRs).

Under the leadership of CEO Peter Randall and COO Hirander Misra, Chi-X Europe became the second-largest market by share of trading for stocks listed on all three bourses. Other so-called MTFs followed Chi-X's lead, seeking to take advantage of new laws aimed at liberalizing the continent's financial markets, but Chi-X remained the most successful.

However, the *Wall Street Journal* had cautioned that MTFs were facing an uncertain future because trading activity slowed drastically through the financial crisis as hedge funds and investment banks, which had exploited the technological advantages of MTFs for their complex trades, withdrew from the market. By contrast, traditional exchanges such as Deutsche Börse AG, London Stock Exchange Group, PLC, and NYSE Euronext typically had a spread of interests. As well as their equity-trading businesses, they generally had derivatives and bond trading, posttrading services, and data and technology units to keep them going when trading slowed, said the *Wall Street Journal*. The MTFs, by contrast, relied exclusively on equity trading for revenue, a problem compounded by their determination to offer lower fees than the exchanges, which meant that they also were operating on thin margins.

Back then, the consensus among their customers was that not all the MTFs would survive.[10] Seeming to confirm this prediction, on December 21, 2009, the London Stock Exchange (LSE) announced plans to take over Turquoise, the loss-making MTF set up by the world's leading investment banks, and merge it with its own Baikal operation to create "a new pan-European trading venture." Turquoise had been set up four years earlier by investment banks that were unimpressed with the cost of trading on the LSE, said *The Guardian*. The deal, which would see the LSE take a 60 percent stake in Turquoise as part of the agreement, would give the LSE control of Turquoise's dark pool trading platform.[11] Furthermore, on April 14, 2010, Turquoise announced that it would expand its trading services into U.S. securities, making it the first European MTF to offer trading during European trading hours of U.S.-listed equities, ETFs, and ADRs (American Depositary Receipts) alongside pan-European trading in 19 markets.

Maintaining its leadership position was already a challenge for Alasdair Haynes, Chi-X Europe's incoming CEO. Randall, the former chief executive who had joined the company from Instinet, had retired on February 27, 2009. Just a few months later, on December 18, in a surprising turn of events, Randall was confirmed as the new CEO at Equiduct, the pan-European trading venue. He had left Chi-X Europe for personal reasons, yet he had been widely tipped to take the helm at Equiduct after Citadel Securities, the market-making and trade-execution division of Citadel Investment Group, took a majority shareholding in July. The platform had been launched in March 2009 by Börse Berlin, which still owns a minority stake.[12] Similarly, Misra, the former COO, had announced his plans on March 14, 2010, to enter the algorithmic trading business and start a technology company. Misra would be the CEO of London-based Algo Technologies, Ltd., which offers market data and trading services.[13]

It would be only a few weeks later, on February 10, 2010, that BATS Europe, Europe's second-largest ATS, announced that it had slashed the time taken to execute an order on its market as it sought to wrest more market share from established exchanges and Chi-X Europe. Ninety-nine percent of trades on BATS Europe were being accepted and acknowledged to the participant in 465 microseconds, CEO Mark Hemsley had said to *Bloomberg Businessweek.* The system upgrade had trimmed so-called latency from 770 microseconds previously and constituted orders sustained at busy times. London-based BATS Europe had been pushing for improved speed after cutting fees for both NYSE Euronext and London Stock Exchange Group, PLC, stocks in 2009 to lure traders.[14]

On the regulatory front, and following on the example set by American counterparts, Timothy Binning, a policy officer in the Securities Markets Unit, announced on February 25, 2010, that the European Commission's 2010 review of MiFID would take into account high-frequency trading. Binning said that the growth of high-frequency trading to 30 to 40 percent of the volume on some European execution venues had raised a number of concerns for the commission. Acknowledging the capacity of high-frequency trading to increase available liquidity through electronic market making and to reduce both market volatility and spreads, Binning nevertheless expressed concerns about the possibility of malfunctioning low-latency trading programs spilling out thousands of erroneous trades into the market. "We are concerned about the risk of a system running amok," he said.

Additional risks cited by Binning included the capacity of European trading venues to handle sharp increases in message traffic and the potential for high-frequency trading to reduce average transaction sizes. Binning added that the European Commission would weigh the impact of high-frequency trading on other market participants, such as traditional retail and institutional investors, in reaching any conclusions on its benefits to the overall market. According to the official, some market participants had reported that their trading infrastructure sometimes was too slow to access prices. Binning said that once a full assessment of the risks and benefits of high-frequency trading had been completed, the commission would first consider whether MiFID's existing provisions were sufficient to regulate the activity before deciding whether additional regulatory intervention was required.[15]

Chi-X Global Path to Asia

Defying expectations for alternative trading venues, Chi-X Global, Inc., went on with ambitious global expansion plans. On March 31, 2010, the firm won preliminary government approval to open Australia's first rival to stock exchange operator, ASX, Ltd. Chi-X Global had been lobbying the government for more than two years to gain entry into the Australian market. The Senate paved the way for rival exchanges when it voted to hand oversight of real-time trading on licensed markets to the Australian Securities and Investments Commission (ASIC), replacing self-regulation that allowed ASX to supervise the nation's main stock exchange. Under arrangements in place since 1998, ASX had been responsible for day-to-day supervision of trading and investigation of possible rules breaches, which it could refer to ASIC, the nation's regulator. Prime Minister Kevin Rudd's government had said that the transfer of the market-supervisor role would enable rival exchanges to be established and that it had received applications from three potential operators.[16]

In part to fend off Chi-X Global's advances, ASX, Ltd., operator of the Australian Stock Exchange, announced on February 18, 2010, a new trading system to be installed later in the year that would slash transaction times and allow more trades to be processed. The Genium platform would cut the average time to execute trades to 250 microseconds from 3 milliseconds, Matthew Gibbs, an ASX spokesman, said. The new system would allow more than 5 million trades per day, Nasdaq OMX Group, Inc., which was providing the platform, said in a statement. ASX's current system permitted 2 million trades, Gibbs said.[17]

The company's expectations were not stopping in Australia. On August 2, 2010, Ronald Gould, CEO at Chi-X Asia-Pacific, a unit of Chi-X Global, said to the *Wall Street Journal* that the group wanted to expand into China, Hong Kong, and India. He also acknowledged that there were ownership and currency restrictions in many other of the major markets in Asia, including China. This did not stop them, though, from launching Chi-X Japan the week before, allowing trade of five Japanese stocks on its platform to five brokerage firms; those stocks included Toyota Motor Corp. and Sumitomo Mitsui Financial Group, Inc.[18]

Japan was an interesting case study for Chi-X Global. There was a clear long-term trend of Tokyo's waning importance in Asian equities markets as bourses such as Shanghai rode the growing clout of their companies and economies. At the peak of Japan's asset bubble in 1989, the Tokyo exchange's market capitalization had accounted for about 40 percent of the value of global markets. Now it was contributing just 7 percent, according to data from the World Federation of Exchanges. On top of that, the Tokyo Stock Exchange had long been derided as one of the world's slowest major bourses.

Despite Tokyo's declining importance, on January 4, 2010, the Tokyo Stock Exchange (TSE) launched a new platform to give it a much-needed shot of speed and to fight off global and domestic rivals such as the upcoming Chi-X Japan; the Arrowhead system, with the ability to handle thousands of orders in the blink of an eye, would make Asia's largest bourse a viable platform for electronic traders and be the answer to the rise of alternative trading platforms, which had been siphoning off volume by offering faster trades and finer price points. Developed by Japanese electronics conglomerate Fujitsu, Ltd., the $145 million system would process trades in 5 milliseconds, 600 times faster than the 2 to 3 seconds needed on the current system and on a par with the New York and London exchanges. The TSE said that the new system would lead to greater use of algorithms and other automated trading strategies. Specifically, Arrowhead should pave the way for more high-frequency trading, where algorithms are used to trade thousands of shares in milliseconds to profit from tiny spreads and market imbalances.

These new developments, it was reported by *The Asian Investor*, prompted several U.S. high-frequency hedge funds, such as D. E. Shaw & Co., to start building up their local desks in order to take advantage of the new infrastructure of the TSE.[19] UBS estimated that about 30 percent of Japanese equity trading was already high-frequency; there was no question that with Chi-X Japan's launch, the participation of high-frequency trading would only increase. In fact, turnover on its platform had already reached 50.2 billion yen in November 2010, trading 98.3 million shares. "One of the most encouraging aspects of our launch to date has been the participation of offshore traders who have adjusted their strategies and algorithms to increase Japanese trading in general and take advantage of trading opportunities created by multiple trading venues. We will continue our efforts to attract these investors and contribute to further liquidity growth in the Japanese market," said Joseph Meyer, representative director of Chi-X Japan.[20]

The Story of Renaissance Technologies

Back in January of 1974, two months after a boy named Ken Griffin turned five, two mathematicians, Shiing Shen Chern and James Simons, a former cold war code breaker, published a paper entitled, "Characteristic Forms and Geometric Invariants," in the *Annals of Mathematics.* This paper involved the discovery and application of certain geometric measurements and resulted in the Chern-Simons form, a theory used in theoretical physics, particularly string theory. In simple terms, the theory provided the tools, known as *invariants,* that mathematicians used to distinguish among certain curved spaces, the kinds of distortions of ordinary space that exist according to Albert Einstein's general theory of relativity. The Chern-Simons form was viewed as important partly because it had proven useful in explaining aspects of another field: string theory. "It turns out these things we invented, Chern-Simons invariants, had their real applications to physics, about which I knew nothing," Simons told the International Association of Financial Engineers in May 2008.[21]

One of these mathematicians, Simons, founded Renaissance Technologies Corp. on July 29, 1982, a firm that later would become one of the most successful hedge fund companies ever. Initially established as a Delaware corporation, Renaissance was among the first to develop a form of trading that used mathematical models and computers to predict markets. In the process, Simons blazed a trail followed by a slew of hedge funds that rely on quantitative strategies, such as D. E. Shaw Group, AQR Capital Management, and Citadel Investment Group.

Nearly Renaissance's entire signature Medallion fund's trading was automated, involving little to no human interference. Computers were programmed to buy and sell assets of all kinds, attempting to predict whether they would rise or fall based on historical patterns. In the fund's early years, Simons focused chiefly on futures, contracts tied to the price of commodities, currencies, and other assets. Medallion's stock-trading operation had become its chief money maker, accounting for more than three-fourths of its returns, said a person familiar with the matter to the *Wall Street Journal*. The firm was known for fast trading, often holding stocks and futures contracts for only minutes or even seconds. Renaissance employed about 90 holders of Ph.D.s to staff the operation, including experts in quantum physics and artificial intelligence.

In late 2007, Renaissance opened Renaissance Institutional Futures Fund (RIFF), focused on futures contracts on bonds, currencies, commodities, and other assets. Like Renaissance Institutional Equities Fund (RIEF), launched in 2005 and focused on stocks of companies on U.S. exchanges only, over a longer time horizon, with the stated goal of beating the Standard & Poor's 500 Stock Index by a few percentage points over a three-year period, RIFF held positions longer than Medallion. After big losses started to hit Renaissance and other quantitative hedge funds, Simons recommended a moderate reduction of the firm's trading positions. Medallion, closed to outside investors, would go on to gain 80 percent in 2008, a disastrous year for the stock market, thanks in part to its focus on taking advantage of short-term swings, both up and down, in all kinds of markets. But the newer funds, which claimed combined assets of about $30 billion (making Renaissance one of the biggest hedge fund operators in the world), experienced disappointing returns over the next few years, leading to a wave of investor withdrawals and combined assets plunging to $6 billion by early 2010.

Simons didn't need to worry about these losses getting in the way of his becoming a legend. Since its inception in 1988, his Medallion fund posted average returns of about 45 percent a year, after fees; moreover, since 1995, it had only one money-losing quarter, slipping 0.5 percent in the first quarter of 1999.[22] Confident in the future, Simons, who had shunned the public eye, retired on January 1, 2010, as chief executive of Renaissance and handed the post to copresidents Bob Mercer and Peter Brown, who would become co-CEOs; Simons remains as a nonexecutive chairman and still has a say in the most important decisions of the firm.[23]

The "Naked Access" Controversy

On January 13, 2010, the SEC voted to propose a new rule that would effectively prohibit broker-dealers from providing customers with "unfiltered" or "naked access" to an exchange or ATS. The SEC's proposed rule required brokers with market access, including those who sponsor customers' access to an exchange, to put in place risk-management controls and supervisory procedures. Among other things, the goal for these procedures was to help prevent erroneous orders, ensure compliance with regulatory requirements, and enforce preset credit or capital thresholds. Broker-dealers use a "special pass" known as their *market participant identifier* (MPID) to electronically access an exchange or ATS and place an order for a customer. Broker-dealers are subject to the federal securities laws as well as the rules of the self-regulatory organizations (SROs) that regulate their operation: FINRA (Financial Industry Regulatory Authority) and MSRB (Municipal Securities Rulemaking Board).

However, these laws and rules did not apply to a non-broker-dealer customer who a broker-dealer provides with an MPID in order to gain individual access to an exchange or ATS. Under this arrangement, known as *direct market access* or *sponsored access*, the customer can place an order that flows directly into the markets without first passing through the broker-dealer' systems and without being prescreened by the broker-dealer in any manner. This type of direct market access arrangement is known as *unfiltered* and *naked access.*

A recent report estimated that naked access accounted for 38 percent of the daily volume for equities traded on the U.S. markets. Erik Lehtis, president of DynamicFX Consulting, admitted the potential for disaster when he said that every time traders are given sponsored direct access to the market, there are people who have the potential to create havoc of one kind or another, which is what regulators are trying to prevent—unpracticed amateurs coming in and trying to mess around in the professionals' game. He favored a kind of access where there would be a filter through capital restraints and checks being imposed externally on the behavior of participants, at least until each of them could demonstrate either capital capacity or the risk and internal controls necessary to prevent them from going absolutely haywire in the market, causing all kinds of damage. "I don't think there is anything wrong with that," Lehtis concluded.[24]

Through sponsored access, especially unfiltered or naked sponsored-access arrangements, there was the potential that financial, regulatory, and other risks associated with the placement of orders would not be managed appropriately. In particular, there was an increased likelihood that customers would enter erroneous orders as a result of computer malfunction or human error, fail to comply with various regulatory requirements, or breach a credit or capital limit. *Forbes* indicated that some high-frequency traders were sending out 1,000 orders a second; thus, in the span of the two minutes it could take to rectify a trading system glitch, a malfunctioning algorithm or careless trader could pump out 120,000 faulty orders; on a $20 stock, that represents a $2.4 billion disaster, *Forbes* cautioned. Without better controls, "the next Long-Term Capital meltdown will happen in a five-minute time period," warned Lime Brokerage in a letter to the SEC.[25] Responding to these concerns, the SEC's proposed rule would require broker-dealers to establish, document, and maintain a system of risk-management controls and supervisory procedures reasonably designed to manage the financial, regulatory, and other risks related to its market access, including access on behalf of sponsored customers.[26]

For Petter Kolm, of the Courant Institute of Mathematical Sciences of New York University, prohibiting naked access was an issue of fairness: "If someone can get it, then there should be a process for others to get it. I think that is an important aspect. Obviously, there needs to be some sort of filter or monitoring process. People who are offered naked access have to go through certain due-diligence process, and a 'certification' has to take place. Additionally, someone is responsible for looking into that on a regular basis. That is a better way of going than simply just not allowing it all together. Then we need to have some form of circuit breakers, either on the naked access level, directly at the different trading venues, or both."[27]

Blazing the Juggernaut Path: GETCO

Former floor traders Stephen Schuler and Dan Tierney recognized at a very early stage the beginning of a paradigm shift in the financial markets and founded Global Electronic Trading Company (GETCO). They believed that technology would fundamentally change the way markets function and usher in a new era of efficiency, transparency, and competition. GETCO would later trade across three continents in four asset classes and on more than 50 markets around the world. Since its founding, the firm has risen to become one of the five biggest traders measured by volume in stocks and other instruments that trade electronically on exchanges, such as Treasury bonds and currency futures.

Tierney was referred to by *Forbes* as a cerebral economist and philosopher who began trading options on the floor of the Chicago Board Options Exchange in 1993. Schuler, a gregarious futures broker, had started out in 1981 on the floor of the Chicago Mercantile Exchange (CME) and eventually opened his own firm. Acquaintances from the clubby world of Chicago's financial markets, they had been researching electronic trading, decided to go into business together, and set up GETCO over a handshake in a small office at the CME on a Friday afternoon in October 1999.

Early on, the firm operated out of space in Schuler's firm barely big enough for a couple of desks and computers. For trading talent, the partners scoured nearby Illinois Institute of Technology in search of skilled video gamers.[28] By 2001, GETCO employed about 20 people and had branched into exchange-traded funds (ETFs).

GETCO heavily depends on the success of its proprietary complex algorithms to help it make money on the transactions more often than not, said the *Wall Street Journal*'s Scott Patterson. On top of that, it also could pick up tiny rebates that exchanges offer to firms willing to take the other side of trading orders.[29]

Building on its successes, on February 11, 2010, GETCO became a NYSE designated market maker (DMM), along with Goldman Sachs, Kellogg Group, Bank of America, and Barclays Capital. GETCO was already a supplemental liquidity provider (SLP) on the NYSE; a market maker on NYSE Arca, the Nasdaq, and BATS exchanges; and consistently among the top five participants by volume on various equities, futures, and options markets.

DMMs were at the center of the NYSE's unique high-tech/high-touch market model and have obligations to maintain an orderly market, quote at the national best bid and offer (NBBO), and facilitate price discovery during openings, closings, and imbalances.[30]

Just a few months later, GETCO would be the designated market maker for General Motors Co.'s wildly successful initial public offering (IPO) at the NYSE. As such, GETCO was to be responsible for buying and selling shares, smoothing trade imbalances, and providing liquidity in return for incentives paid by the exchange.[31]

The success of GETCO highlighted what a powerful financial and technology hotbed Chicago had become. Infinium Capital Management, the Chicago firm that placed its first trade on September 10, 2001, had just absorbed Fox River Partners, LLC, of Chicago on January 20, 2010, in a consolidation move that would combine one of the leading private global trading houses handling a vast range of derivatives with one of the foremost traders specializing in the equity options market. Infinium had grown rapidly to embrace high-volume electronic trading and market making in derivatives, metals, grains, energies, financial instruments, and other products; its staff of over 250 employees then was expanding its reach into Asian and Pacific Rim commodities markets as well.[32]

High-Frequency Trading in New York Courts

After shunning the media for many years, high-frequency trading became a daily feature on the major networks. Goldman Sachs had been on the news too as the Wall Street juggernaut that quickly recovered from the financial crisis, thanks to taxpayers' largesse, and was already churning extraordinary profits, which many attributed to its proprietary trading. Therefore, it was a match made in heaven between the financial giant everybody loved to hate (it had been referred as a "great vampire squid wrapped around the face of humanity" by *Rolling Stone*'s Matt Taibbi[33]) and the trading practice in vogue.

The media loved to speak about Sergey Aleynikov, the former Goldman Sachs computer programmer responsible for developing computer programs to support high-frequency trading in the commodities and equities markets who had been arrested and charged in the matter on July 3, 2009. He pleaded not guilty on February 18, 2010, to charges that he stole computer codes used in Goldman Sachs's proprietary high-frequency trading program. Aleynikov had been indicted the week before on charges of theft of trade secrets, transportation of stolen property in interstate and foreign commerce, and unauthorized computer access.

Prosecutors from the U.S. attorney's office in Manhattan alleged that Aleynikov, on his last day at Goldman Sachs in June 2009, had transferred substantial portions of Goldman's proprietary computer code for its high-frequency trading platform to an outside computer server in Germany. Aleynikov, who had worked at Goldman as a computer programmer from May 2007 to June 2009, had been hired by Teza Technologies, LLC, to develop a similar platform to engage in high-frequency trading, prosecutors said. He was suspended by the company after his arrest and subsequently terminated.[34]

Around the same time, April 19, 2010, FBI agents arrested Samarth Agrawal, a citizen of India and former Société Générale (SocGen) trader, on the charge of theft of a computer code used in high-frequency proprietary trading in the bank's New York office.

Agrawal "without authorization, copied, printed, and removed from the offices of a financial institution proprietary computer code for the financial institution's high-frequency trading business, with the intent to use that code for the economic benefit of himself and others," the FBI agent had written.[35] Agrawal resigned from the bank in November 2009, according to the complaint.

He had joined as an analyst in the high-frequency trading group in March 2007 and was promoted to trader in April 2009.

A statement from SocGen revealed that it had discovered the apparent theft: "Société Générale conducted an internal investigation and discovered the apparent misappropriation of confidential computer code developed and used by the firm in its high-frequency proprietary trading operation in New York," spokesman Jim Galvin said in a statement. "SG promptly informed federal law enforcement authorities and has been cooperating fully with the investigation. No client information or funds were involved in the incident."[36]

A *New York Times* article on July 23 brought a significant amount of attention to an industry that had tried to stay under the radar. While we know of many cases of industrial espionage, the extra attention firms such as Goldman Sachs put on one of their programmers' unauthorized code download piqued the media's interest and suspicion that something special was under the hood. Citadel's high-frequency trading had brought the bacon to the firm when its bigger funds were floundering; therefore, there was no reason not to suspect similar results at Goldman Sachs motivated its zealousness. According to Manoj Narang, president of Tradeworx, the "dark age" for high-frequency trading had started.

CHAPTER 6

Meet the Speed Traders: Peter van Kleef

"My ultimate motivation would have to be the challenge. There are a lot of smart people in the financial markets, and to come up with something they haven't thought of is a formidable challenge that never gets boring. In my private life, success is if my family is happy. I have a wife and two kids, boy and girl, so I'm very lucky in that respect. On a business level, success to me means figuring something out—if something works that didn't come easy and didn't just fall into my lap."

Peter van Kleef is CEO of Lakeview Arbitrage and a partner with Lakeview Capital Market Services. In the past, van Kleef directly managed quantitative trading departments and proprietary hedge-fund-related investment products for Salomon Brothers, Cooper Neff, HypoVereinsbank, and Credit Lyonnais, among others. He has more than 15 years of experience in the development and running of sophisticated automated trading operations. He is a well-known consultant to the investment community with regard to trading, risk management, and operational and strategic issues. Van Kleef is also widely regarded as one of the world's leading authorities on sophisticated automated trading operations and on complex arbitrage strategies involving volatility and/or algorithmic modeling/trading.

Interest in Finance and Technology

"To be honest," says van Kleef, "I do not recall any experience that provided the initial spark for my career path. I guess people always expect there to be a specific key event that then determines one's life. Not for me. I think, if anything, it is that I have always been interested in many things. To be able to step back and look outside the box seems helpful. What my parents did for me that helps me now is they showed me a lot of different things and encouraged curiosity and creativity. Of course, they also showed me the value of hard work, not giving up, and persistence."

Van Kleef started becoming interested in computers when they were still relatively new. The dealers were offering trials before people would buy because the first Mac and IBM PCs were very expensive. So he went for the trial, and ever since then, he has been hooked on what could be done with computers. His interest in finance came later when he started college.

"I became interested in the markets by following IBM, Apple, and Sun Microsystems. Those were the first names I traded with the little money I had. Back then, I was using a very naive process for investing. I thought that if a company was making great, novel products, its stock should go up. As it turns out, it is not always that simple. I started using options early in my trading to get more leverage on what little capital I had and had some pretty severe drawdowns. It definitely helped me to understand that you can be right about direction, seemingly choose the right product to make the bet, and still lose money. Sun, for example, was a visionary with 'The network is the computer,' but the company was too far ahead of its time."

Education and Professional Beginnings

Van Kleef has a business degree in finance, banking and investments from Munich Polytechnic University and an MBA with a finance major from the Owen Graduate School of Business at Vanderbilt University, Nashville, Tennessee. His first work experience was trading for Salomon Brothers, a great experience, he remembers. He was definitely jumping in at the deep end and made market maker for the German DAX (Deutscher Aktien Index, German stock index, a blue-chip stock market index consisting of the 30 major German companies trading on the Frankfurt Stock Exchange) on his first day in the office. That world doesn't exist anymore, he laments.

"I had started playing with tech stocks while at the university. Then I went for my MBA and applied for trading positions after that. Initially, I worked for small but cutting-edge firms such as Cooper Neff (ultimately acquired by BNP Paribas in 1995) and

Transoptions, then some large banks, and finally set up my own shop. Pretty much all the firms I've ever worked for were engaged in high-frequency trading, especially the ones I worked for early in my career. It never really crossed my mind why someone would want to trade any other way. It is just so much more efficient. This is why, if there is some advice that I can give to people considering career options in the industry, I would suggest getting an account at a broker that gives a simple and free API [Application Programming Interface] and start writing your own strategies. If possible, join forces with some friends. Trading is best learned by doing. Nothing beats hands-on experience. By setting up alone or, even better, in a team, one learns a great deal. The new technologies empower individuals and make them competitive with large institutions. Once something is working, scalability is easy from a technology point of view. Trying to apply solutions from other fields of science and research is also a good start. I would suggest looking at what problems have been solved in other industries and how they relate to and can be applied to trading. Be creative. If you join a company, look for small and nimble firms that are at the cutting edge. With more than 50 to 100 people, it gets difficult to stay at the cutting edge."

Staying at the cutting edge of his profession takes a big toll on van Kleef in terms of time spent with his family; he travels extensively to South Asia, where many investment firms and startups are increasingly interested in high-frequency trading. Notes van Kleef: "Whenever possible, I try to balance work with some sort of physical exercise. This is something that every trader will appreciate, because it is really needed to balance your life. I like to play golf and tennis, and in winter, I go skiing. There are no regular workdays. Some weeks I travel a lot and have lots of meetings, and others I am stuck in front of an array of computer screens. Generally, I like to get up late and work late. I am a night owl. This is definitely not great if your local markets are opening early."

Lakeview and High-Frequency Trading

Lakeview Arbitrage is a pure systematic relative trading firm that trades fully automated for its own account. Lakeview Capital Market Services (LCMS), its consulting arm, provides a wide range of services designed to make customers more successful in the global financial markets. There is no exchange of data, strategies, or any other information or staff between the two to avoid any potential conflict of interest. LCMS is able to guide customers from their first steps to the last tweaks for their most sophisticated strategies and infrastructure issues. Services range from intermediation to hands-on support and custom information technology (IT) development for customers, assisting them in solving challenging issues. LCMS places a high value on the sustainability and adaptability of the services and solutions that it provides to its customers.

"Back in the day, we started our high-frequency trading operation after a couple of years of development work and seven figures of investment. Now it would be a signature and $10,000 to $20,000 per month to be able to compete.

"At Lakeview, we pretty much trade anywhere there is electronic trading on a regulated exchange. We offer managed accounts in Lakeview Capital Market Services GmbH and specific, systematic executions. I think the future will indeed be managed accounts, with transsparency, costs, and liquidity being the main reasons.

"We employ about 10 to 12 people. Recruiting is not easy, and we have had bad experiences with staff in jurisdictions where enforcement is sometimes difficult. We now have staff only in G7 countries and Switzerland. Cost is much higher but so is productivity and quality. Compensation is largely based on performance. Contacts with universities and the high-tech industry, as well as trading communities, are the main sources of talent for us.

"High-frequency traders can achieve consistent profits irrespective of market condition by identifying opportunities that the competition doesn't see and certainly not by running the strategies that are well publicized and where competition is fierce. Good risk management is also a key point; bad and insufficient risk management is the reason for most problems and the bad rep high-frequency trading has.

"Visibility of the order flow and institutional orders is very helpful, but it is not all-important, more of a very nice to have, I would say. In the end, large institutional orders find their way to market and leave their imprint. On the other hand, low latency is very important for high-frequency trading firms, of course, but that alone doesn't make you any money. Similarly, colocation and proximity to the exchanges are very important at the high end; it will become the standard without which competing will be very hard; not quite there yet, but it seems to be coming.

"Let me give you an actual example; if you look back in the history of algorithmic trading, we have seen a version of the speed race before in the early 1990s, when the markets first became electronic and participants started to compete for speed in order to take advantage of arbitrage opportunities. For instance, we were trading in the German market from Switzerland, which is pretty far away, maybe 1,000 kilometers; at that moment, we were the fastest because we were the only one. However, at one point, we weren't the fastest anymore, so we decided to do something about it; let's move closer to the market. So we moved to the country where the market was located, and for a time, it was fine because, supposedly, the competition was another company that was located abroad. Then those guys moved as well, and the only thing that would help was to move to the city in which the exchange was located. That was working for a while and then, again, stopped working, so we had to move within the city closer to the exchange because it was really the physical distance to the market. Since that didn't work anymore either, we asked the exchange if we could move our machine to its space. The exchange took two days to consider it and then accepted. So that is how thinks change; it is not as though we haven't seen some form of speed race before. At that point, it was about spending more and more money on computers. I can remember we bought very expensive computers, for almost half a million euros; if you imagine what kind of computer you are getting for with that, it's not your average laptop; that was a pretty heavy machine. In the end, though, that didn't help either. There was always someone that would be a fraction of a millisecond faster than you. So it will always take a lot of money to be the fastest one in the market; however, even the fastest infrastructure can have technical problems.

"It is time for people to stop competing for speed and start producing alpha. Sometimes we have three or four customers who tell us they are the fastest in the market; we look at the statistics, and they are not even in the top five. So why do they think they are the fastest? Because they are slightly more aggressive than other participants; many people are running similar strategies, and in the end, it turns out that the people who think they are the fastest do so only because they are the only ones; they are the most aggressive. Everyone could be paying 21; they are paying 21.10; of course, they are the fastest because they are the only ones paying 21.10; the other ones don't want to pay that. Of course, you are going to be the fastest. In conclusion, a lot of the profits that are sustainable usually will come from the strategy and not necessarily from technology. Technology is a big enabler indeed; you know you have to get the technology in order to compete. Just because some people have the fastest machines doesn't necessarily mean that they will make much money.

"Leverage is a key driver because returns are quite low but consistent if no leverage is employed. Some strategies maybe make 4 basis points at a cost of 2 basis points. By using leverage and a lot of transactions, that return can turn into a 100 or 200 percent return a year on capital with very little risk. The overall profit largely depends only on the number of trades that can be done because the average profit per trade is nearly certain. I don't know many other strategies that, if run well, consistently range about 50 percent return per year and above. We are not in the business to rate ourselves; high-frequency trading is very profitable, if done right. That much is sure."

Misconceptions about High-Frequency Trading

Van Kleef strongly disagrees with the opinion that high-frequency traders are irresponsible and greedy speculators who are out to trick and hurt other market participants. Most in the high-frequency trading field try to make fairly certain, consistent, and replicable profits by running a much disciplined business and are far from speculation, he says.

"With all the market fragmentation that is happening, they would keep prices in line and make sure everyone gets equal pricing. Due to efficient arbitraging of price discrepancies, it is thanks to high-frequency trading that prices stay in line across venues and liquidity is routed to the most efficient venue."

Most people who complain about high-frequency trading are not even in the business and do not even understand how it works, he complains. For him, there is a lot of envy and fear that drive the discussion; the result is mostly a discussion based on polemics rather than facts. The complainers should spend some time learning about what they are talking about, he thinks. He gives the example of some sophisticated retail investors who are already running high-frequency trading strategies. There will be more, he says. "The benefits are compelling; if you can reduce market impact and improve executions, it is easier to beat the competition."

For van Kleef, the main risk for the industry is that there are many players who should not be in the market, employing unsophisticated technology and strategies that give high-frequency trading the bad reputation. The established leaders in the high-frequency trading space are rarely in the spotlight and also usually are not the ones who cause spectacular accidents that disrupt the markets, he says.

"It has become so easy to get into the field, and publicity has been such that it starts to attract people who should not be in it. Fortunately, the market is a great equalizer and regulator, eliminating the weak sooner or later. This may not come without the occasional disruption, however."

The Future of High-Frequency Trading

"High-frequency trading is actually becoming a commodity because nowadays you can buy the necessary infrastructure rather than having to build it. Ultra-high-frequency trading is where people still do a lot of custom work. The next step from software in this area is hardware acceleration. It will be very challenging for regulators to understand what is good and bad. If done right, the automation certainly is in the interest of the end investor, even though not all of them realize that.

"Most strategies these days are trend-following. The masses love to follow the trend. Just read any behavioral finance book. Bad algorithms have no common sense and get easily caught in destructive loops such as: I sell, so the market goes down; I sell more, it goes down even more; the faster I sell, the faster it goes down, and the more money I make. Of course, this doesn't take into account that at one point it becomes ridiculous and just a self-feeding frenzy. This is what happened on May 6. No miracle, no mystery. Just good old herd behavior accelerated by technology. Normally, people running such algorithms disappear as soon as they get wiped out. The worst thing that market operators and regulators can do is to protect them by canceling their trades. The trades should have not been allowed in the first place.

"Part of what will determine the future of the industry, of course, is what regulatory changes legislators and the SEC [Securities and Exchange Commission] will introduce. The brief market crash of May 6, which sent the Dow Jones Industrial Average down nearly 700 points in minutes before recovering, shone a spotlight on the effects of having deeply fragmented markets in the United States. In fact, the SEC started a review of the country's market structure in 2009 and proposed rules to make dark pools more transparent and to ban flash orders.

"Regulatory changes that might impact the growth of high-frequency trading include publicized bans on naked access, short selling, and flash orders; there will be lots of ill-informed regulation shooting from the hip and following public sentiment and outcry rather that fact and necessity. I hope that the trend is reversed soon. I think at least some regulators are now trying to make an effort to get educated before enacting inefficient and rather disruptive regulation. There are many suggestions I would have for them, including tapered circuit breakers (warning, slowing down, cutting off), pretrade risk monitoring on the exchange side, transparency with regard to order originator beyond broker, smaller required size and holding period for market-maker quotes, and clear rules that eliminate the possibility of missed trades. In general, I would suggest more responsibility on the side of exchanges and market operators.

"More traditional investment managers will continue expanding into high-frequency trading because there are many compelling benefits for them to do so. Spreads and inefficiencies in the markets are still quite high, and taking advantage of that gives an edge over the competition. In general, the investment business is moving toward industrialization. So anything that adds efficiency and reduces costs has to be at least interesting."

In the future of high-frequency trading, van Kleef sees faster access, better technology, more safety owing to better market rules and regulations, more volume, and better liquidity. There are many trends that will facilitate this progression, including hardware acceleration and the use of social networking and general Internet content, and according to van Kleef, the future is bright indeed.

CHAPTER 7

The Technology Race in High-Frequency Trading

High-frequency trading has become the most sophisticated arms race out there; in order to process orders at speed down from seconds to milliseconds, then down from milliseconds to hundreds of microseconds, and now from hundreds of microseconds to single microseconds, firms have become adept at extracting even minimal efficiency gains so that their market-making strategies have a chance to succeed. In this field, the complexity seems to be endless because modern technology availability is increasing. Technology is getting faster, so people can do more than at earlier times.

Racers in the high-frequency trading world first include people who used to trade on the floor; about a decade ago, they turned from floor trading to computerized trading. The second group includes the "new" people in this industry, who in most cases have either mathematics or physics backgrounds or quant experience required to build sophisticated trading models; they are trained to trade using the firm strategies.

Jitesh Thakkar, president of Edge Financial Technologies, categorizes the technology requirements into three different parts. First of all, there is networking, and this includes the telephone lines, routers, and switches; facilities; and all the hardware. Second, there is the hardware, which includes the machines and uploading and messaging systems. Third would be the actual algorithm. Most traders have an idea of what they want to achieve; the technology experts will review their requests in detail and then implement them into a system and test it.[1]

As Peter van Kleef mentioned in Chapter 6, there are a few important elements that are required to implement an effective high-frequency trading platform. First, a reliable and sufficiently fast data input source is needed; in this regard, there are a numbers of vendors that provide either raw or processed data that can be connected to a firm's systems. James Leman, principal of Westwater Corp., agrees that high-speed market data provisioning is extremely important, as well as the ultra-high-speed connectivity to the marketplace through the broker. A published market data aggregator capability is also an important component, he says, adding that going to native codes such as ITCH[2] and OUCH[3] and some of the protocols that are used as opposed to a more standardized code that other people are using is going to provide an important speed advantage.

Second, a robust and sufficiently fast market access is required; more and more exchanges are offering superfast access, in particular, those using the Genium platform, Nasdaq OMX's commercial exchange technology offering. It has been announced that Singapore Exchange Limited (SGX), implementing a solution from the Nasdaq, will become the fastest exchange in the world as of early 2011, offering average order response times of

90 microseconds door to door. According to Leman, firms that want to take advantage of these speeds require complex event stream processing capabilities currently being introduced into the market by a number of providers to help firms analyze their data flows. He says that the amount of information that is flowing is tremendous because of the speed of the changing of the messages and the canceling and replacing, so all of that goes into just how well high-frequency traders can run their shop. Brokers are reaching challenging points too, he adds, when they cope with just simple direct market access (DMA) and direct strategy access (DSA) types of strategies coming through their systems, reason to think what will the next two or three customers and the next two or three strategies will do with their infrastructure.

Leman shares the story of an organization he worked with: "They didn't pay attention to their network, they had a tremendous number of orders going through and exchange messages coming back, and they were thrown offline because their algorithmic server and the way it was pulling in the data (and not dealing with the data essentially) were hobbling the network." This is why he stresses that every dimension in the organization is important, not just how well the algorithms are running and the marketplace connectivity.

The third element for van Kleef is low enough transaction, clearing, and processing costs, as well as a sufficiently effective and efficient processing and verification capability. Importantly, too, is high enough volume and profit potential of the strategy in proportion to the expense to achieve the preceding. This can be thought of as cost-benefit analysis applied to high-frequency trading.

According to Thakkar, monitoring tools are becoming an important part of high-frequency trading because the system usually requires extremely high speeds: "There are many tools out there to monitor network latency, operating system latency, and application latency. But there are not many tools that could monitor all. Monitoring latency is very important because it will directly influence profits. This is why every high-frequency trading shop would like to keep latency to zero to make sure that their orders are profitable. And a lot of exchanges have backups so that if the server fails or something crashes, they can still continuing trading."

Other important elements are an integrated risk and trading system and robust models and risk-simulation capability. Andrew Kumiega, director of quality for Infinium Capital Management, sees a trend of more people building their own risk systems. "Someone uses services from some little high-frequency trading shops, but at the end of the day, they want to start their own; firms then will go on to order the connection from vendors. They will have a shopping list stating what they have purchased before and what they need now that is different. Everyone used MicroHedge in the 1990s, but then they started to find out that this software does not work. So everyone started to build a system on their own; more accurately, they made changes on the system they previously ordered. At the end of the day, they could hardly tell which part was a vendor's and which part was what they built. Vendors found this situation and made changes in their business. Instead of saying, 'Buy our system, and you can only use our system,' they claimed, 'Buy ours and change what you want.' And that's how a lot of firms are evolving, starting with one system they ordered and ending up with their own."

Finally, it's important to use an open platform that allows for development or at least integration. Kumiega sees that most people want their server in-house and their algorithms in-house: "There is giant fear about it that someone is coming to steal my business, and this is why there are not many people talking about it. All algorithm shops are panicked that someone will know what they are doing. In this case, very few people would like to put his or her algorithms anywhere close to what he or she thinks is a big shop. Firms fear this because a small fish will be eaten by some big ones."[4]

Other Startup Considerations

Proven personnel and developed strategies are the most important considerations to start in high-frequency trading. As Leman sees it, "Personnel can move from one type of organization that has a lot of capabilities and a lot of technology to a smaller organization, and that's a challenge. A lot of people get used to [a certain level of personnel], especially in larger shops, and then they migrate to smaller shops, even though they have been in a startup operation; so one of the things I think people have to consider is the mix of people—how many people will there be in the organization? I have talked to two- or three-person shops that are running and are making money doing high volumes of trading, but they have different characteristics from some of the larger shops that have multiple strategies running at the same time."

The algorithmic strategies are important, he adds, because many traditional buy-side firms are taking algorithms that are created and now being customized by their brokers; what is really going to be the order of the day are shops that are doing customized algorithms and essentially building to suit. The quality issue is going to very important too because, he adds, these algorithms already have gone through at least three generations up to the present, and they are going to be moving forward both in terms of speed and sensitivity; each market is different, each product area is different, and reusability is not really the big thing. Do firms have people who are thinking about it the right way in terms of the process of developing it?

Finally, low latency is extremely important in any provider that high-frequency trading firms are using or any broker they are forced to go through because of market regulations. Obviously, there are a number of players and providers in the marketplace that are trying to sell services and that are trying to sell their technology, their tool kit, and their ability to help firms to cut to the chase more quickly. Leman warns buyers to beware because the way the world goes forward may not be as simple as build or buy but to blend the best of both worlds.

A Methodology for Developing High-Frequency Trading Systems

Mutual funds, hedge fund industries, banks, and proprietary trading firms are now being forced to quickly research, test, and implement speedy trade selection and execution systems. Kumiega and Ben Van Vliet, lecturer at the Illinois Institute of Technology, developed a step-by-step methodology for such development.[5] Their methodology (called *K|V*) addresses the needs of the institutional trading and hedge fund industries for development, presentation, and evaluation of high-speed trading and investment systems.

Kumiega explains the methodology by stages. In stage 1, before firms even start building, they should ask themselves how they are going to monitor a successful algorithm. High-frequency traders need to fully articulate the business logic and quantitative methods and, over the iterative research process, plan each loop that will require team members to redefine goals and set boundaries for that research. Firms can quickly build several generations in order to evaluate whether a particular idea warrants further investigation and to promote risk-based iterative development. Thus, if firms look at this as a machine to build, they will measure everything they can because collecting data for the algorithm is free.

Important measures would be mean profit and median profit, standard deviation of return, Sharp ratio, and winning and losing trades. Firms also would want to know, on average, how many days they are winners and how many days they are losers. If that shifts, something has broken in their machine. The profit and loss (P&L) may not even slip, but if they start having a low pickup ratio, something has changed in their machine. Thus, in stage 1, the process capability index (C_{pk})[6] is pushing up. These ideas obviously come from manufacturing, and the question is whether their algorithms are working within their current levels. Firms would want their machine to work within their plus or minus targets.

For stage 2, firms build a customized database of historical data and purchase or build a software tool that allows for proper testing of a given strategy; the required data may either not exist at all or be prohibitively expensive based on the prospective returns of the trading strategy. The next step is to develop data-cleaning methods—a data transformation management system (DTMS) that will scan data for errors and irregularities. That being said, the system will need to prove its validity even when confronted with the raw data because the cleaning process may eliminate market nuances that could affect its profitability. Kumiega warns that firms need to think through the use of "clean" or "dirty" data; of course, most firms at startup don't have dirty data, so he recommends calling vendors and asking for really dirty data to test their algorithms.

Firms need to consider machine control theory in their development process, controlling the algorithm outputs by looking at their standard deviations. When the algorithm goes out of the range, firms are going to shut up the algorithm. Every single main manufacturing plant shuts off if it gets 3 standard deviations away from normal. Firms will need to perform algorithm benchmarking with sample data and use statistical process control to check for ambiguity in trading algorithm output. There are important indications of a system out of control or in an ambiguous state: any single measurement above or below the upper or lower control limits, five consecutive measurements moving in the same direction up or down, two measurements greater than 2 standard deviations from the mean, three measurements more than 1.5 standard deviations from the mean, and seven consecutive measurements on one side of the mean.

Kumiega makes the case that even a system that is profitable can be killed. While some traders may want to spend a couple of million dollars to show how this system works in the real world, hiring programmers, buying real data feed, and incurring other development expenses, there are grounds to kill a system if it doesn't produce the right type of money, avoiding investing in the next stage of development.[7]

Finally, firms need to check performance and probationary trade—in other words, shadow trade the algorithm. According to Kumiega, "If you test for a week, then you probably could assume that you have a week's stability. If you test for two years, you've got two years' stability. There are products out there that allow you to get tick data and try your strategies out. It is expensive. Let's go back to the most important question: In what business do you want to be? If you want to be in a super-high-frequency, low-latency, thousands-of-trades business, then $1 million is not much money. If you want to be in an automated order-maker business, then it is a huge amount of money. So take the question seriously—In what business do you want to be, and why do you think you can beat other competitors? This is really going to determine how long and why you need backtesting."

For many people, backtesting is paramount to the successful deployment of even extremely well-thought-out high-frequency trading strategies. Leman confirms that it goes without saying that there needs to be historical backtesting: "There needs to be ongoing testing, and as results are presented, you need to make sure that the results you're seeing are the results you want to see, not something unexplainable. You want to make sure that things are going according to expectations."

Backtesting has its limitations, though. For Thakkar, backtesting is tough to complete if your strategy depends on latency, market data, and timing. One can tutor the strategy to get a profitable result. But once you put it into practice, maybe there will be someone else providing liquidity before you and getting the same results, he says. For backtesting, what people usually do is turn on the strategy live but not send live results. Thakkar has worked with high-frequency traders who were trading Eurodollars in the pits, now electronically, who don't backtest at all. Instead, he says, they build the tools with a lot of controls so that even they have a black box or gray box on which they always have their fingers so that they can start a pretty good strategy very quickly. Thakkar suggests that traders who intend to compete with the big firms should get cutting-edge machines that incorporate Monte Carlo simulation and the Black-Scholes option pricing model.

For stage 3, teams fully define the functionalities and performance requirements of the trading/investment system. The specification documents allow the team of hardware engineers and programmers to quickly build the system with the correct functionalities and to the proper specifications. By the time a product team reaches this stage, most, if not all, of the groundwork for successful deployment has already been laid. The requirements have been gathered and thoroughly tested in previous stages. Any design errors that have been discovered or changes that have been made to the investment strategy from this point on would require a return to stage 1 for rework and retesting.

Finally, in stage 4, firms will develop reports that present the portfolio statistics, performance metrics, and risk calculations and provide documentation of the attribution of gains and losses. Risk control techniques should help the team to understand whether or not the system is working within specifications and in conformance with the backtesting and/or a benchmark. Markets are stochastic, and trading/investment system performance will be stochastic as well.

Kumiega suggests that firms ask themselves if the system is working the way it was set up in stages 1, 2, and 3. Is the distribution the same? Are all the measurements the same? When the algorithm goes out of the range, it can be said that the machine is no longer working its specification. This doesn't mean that the algorithm is going to make money or not going to make money. The machine is just no longer working. Once a system is deemed to be out of control, it needs to be fixed. There are a few ways to fix the problem, starting with the implementation of containment actions. Other options include checking for data latency, checking for a new competitor with a better algorithm, releasing a newer algorithm, and redesign of the algorithm to outperform the new competitor.

Kumiega concludes by saying that any high-frequency trading system is a complex machine that should be built and managed according to process engineering theory. A hybrid development cycle using different tools for different development stages is optimal for quantitative finance, which requires a specialized process owing to the large amount of cutting-edge research and development (R&D), time pressures, and cross-functional teams with specialized skills. Finally, Kumiega says, the next life-cycle stage in quantitative finance is the quality stage, owing to the fact that as all industries mature, they eventually have to focus on process quality to produce goods and services that win wars.

"Winning wars" means picking the right battles to fight and walking out of battles that are sure to be lost. Firms can't expect to win all the battles that are being fought in the high-frequency trading landscape. Only the big firms will be able to deploy enough resources to build the fastest systems because they will be looking for the speed advantage. While significant profits will be captured using latency-sensitive strategies, there will be an open field for firms that won't be 100 percent reliant on speed. This is what makes the field of high-frequency trading interesting. Speed is not the answer, just a facilitator to certain strategies; for others, it won't matter as much.

CHAPTER 8

Meet the Speed Traders: Adam Afshar

"We are adamant about not allowing any humans anywhere near our execution system. The execution system has to be an adaptive system."

Adam Afshar, president of Hyde Park Global Investments, was always interested in technology. He was born in Iran, and he grew up in Europe. Eventually, he moved to the United States to attend university. Afshar, who is married and has one son, went to Wofford College, a small institution in South Carolina, for his undergraduate degree in economics. Although he studied economics, he wasn't really interested in the financial markets.

"Wofford was a great experience. The school had about 1,200 students, and the teachers were wonderful. Later, I did my MBA at the University of Chicago, and the place was buzzing with ideas and intellect. For me, it was a life-changing and transformational experience, one akin to going from being color-blind to suddenly being able to see all sorts of colors."

After graduating, Afshar began working at Bear Stearns, and it was there that he realized that he could find trend patterns using quantitative methods.

"It took me a while to believe that the markets were more or less efficient under normal circumstances and to realize that the analysts at most firms provided no value and sometimes a negative value. My first attempt at using the computer was to build a system to help traders have better information faster to enable them or their portfolio managers to make better decisions, a sort of hybrid system where the computers are helping the humans. But, in less than a year, I realized that discretionary human participation in selection, portfolio management, or trading was so deleterious that no amount of computer power or intellectual algorithms could mitigate it."

Hyde Park Global Investments, Afshar's firm, is an investment and trading firm that has developed an artificial intelligence system built primarily on genetic algorithms and other evolutionary models to identify mispricings, arbitrage, and patterns for many electronic financial markets and the robotic platform to monetize the opportunities. The firm, which trades its own capital so far, potentially will accept investments from outside sources.

Is the High-Frequency Trading Field Level?

"We think it is a fair and reasonable question to ask how capitalism can be built off the back of high-frequency traders/speculators," Afshar says. "The answer is that these traders/speculators are the ones that are creating the liquidity in the market. Although the markets are a capital origination source, their principal utility, we will argue, is to provide liquidity. We would argue that even the players outside the public markets, for example, private equity investors, are also benefiting from the participation of the short-term players."

For Afshar, there are several misconceptions about high-frequency trading; for example, there is a fundamental lack of understanding that high-frequency trading is a method or tool and not a strategy.

"The controversy we read in the press is not really about high-frequency trading but about technology; it is just easier to target high-frequency trading than to be against technology. A few years ago, big Wall Street firms and hedge funds had some institutional advantages. For example, they had information that gave them an advantage over other investors in terms of their ability to transact at lower costs than other investors. Today, technology has very much created a meritocracy in the markets, where the smartest investor will win, not the investor with the biggest wallet. The real question is what is it about technology that has created this meritocracy/democratization of the market? The answer, in our view, is that technology has lowered friction costs, which included transaction costs (commission and slippage, etc.), cost of acquisition of information, and the time value of money. This reduction in friction costs has leveled the playing field so that a small firm in Atlanta, Georgia, can now compete with and beat the biggest Wall Street firms at their own game. This reduction in friction costs also had some surprising consequences, one of which is the ability to minimize the abandonment cost so that when the computer has identified a potential return, the computer will seek it very fast (in milliseconds) and can just as fast abandon it for a better relative return because there is very little cost or penalty for this shift. The new potential return can be on the other side of the world. Computers can monitor thousand of companies' bonds and commodities and seek potential returns with less and less friction cost and incredible speed."

Model-Driven Systems with No Human Intervention

Hyde Park Global Investments trades in many asset classes that have an electronic market. "We are naturally very sensitive to regulations and liquidity. Regardless of the market that we are trading in, we will trade only where we can keep human discretionary intervention at zero percent."

Afshar is indeed very emphatic when he says that, at Hyde Park Global Investments, when he talks about artificial intelligence and robotic trading, he means a trading platform that does not allow any human intervention, unlike traditional investment operations, which are unlikely to adapt a robotic trading system; they typically believe that there is a type of knowledge and intuition that cannot be replaced by machines, and an insurmountable wall goes up for them that no amount of evidence can overcome when the idea of robotic trading comes into play.

"It's very important to stress this point because if the system allows human discretion at any level (idea generation, portfolio management, or trading) and your machine does not have the human discretionary elements modeled correctly in its learning algorithm (which we claim is not possible at this time), what you are left with is simply a quantitative trader that uses certain calculations to assist his or her trading. It becomes difficult or even impossible to assess whether the success or failure was due to the calculations, formula, or algorithms. Although we can argue on the pros and cons of humans as traders, we have to agree that this method is not and cannot be scientific. It is not scientific because it is not possible to backtest a model that allows any discretionary human intervention. For example, if you have computers that are generating trades, but the execution is done by humans, then we would argue that you cannot determine whether the success or failure of the system was due to its robust artificial intelligence or to a very good trader, and there is no way of testing and duplicating the results. Therefore, we would argue that any backtesting becomes essentially void."

Afshar notes that his firm manages a number of models, including some in the arbitrage category, that work in microseconds and therefore require extreme high-frequency trading. In addition to arbitrage, Afshar notes that with the help of scientists from Carnegie Mellon University, his team has developed a pattern-prediction model: "We now have pattern-prediction models, for the U.S. and some European markets, text analytics models that are based on machine-readable text, and long-short models also based on text analytics. None of those models allows any human intervention; again, these are purely robotic trading systems."

On longer-term programs such as text-analytics trading or pattern-recognition trading, where there is a bigger margin and longer holding periods, high frequency and low latency are less critical. Afshar believes that low latency and high frequency nevertheless are pivotal in the execution part. Why? Because even if one has a trade that one is holding for a day, that trade needs to be executed without a human trader in an adaptive algorithmic system, and an adaptive algorithmic system requires a very high-speed execution system based on extremely low-latency data; otherwise, one is trading based on stale data.

"This is important because your models have to trade based on what they have learned, and the actual trading and the models have to be very similar. If there is any degradation in data in real trading, then that means that what you have learned in your model is not really applicable to live trading. When you are involved with robotic trading, your real trades have to be very similar to your model trades; otherwise, you have a model that is not necessarily executable or monetizable. We feel that even if your models are longer-term holding, the execution system has to be high frequency and low latency. Moreover, the execution should be decided by a computer based on an algorithm; this algorithm is not always going to be right (nor is the human trader going to be always right), but at least you get feedback that you can use to correct your algorithm. You are not going to get that with a human trader. This is why we are adamant about not allowing any humans anywhere near our execution system. In the robotic world, the execution system has to be an adaptive system. If the system is not adaptive based on artificial intelligence, then it is a dumb system that needs human intervention to constantly tweak it, like a cruise control on a car that the driver has to constantly adjust for up and down hills."

When Afshar says he runs a 100 percent robotic trading firm, this means that he does not hire any portfolio managers, stock analysts, or traders. In the past, Hyde Park Global Investments primarily has recruited Ph.D.s in mathematics, statistics, computer science, and machine learning directly from the university. Having trading experience is irrelevant and rarely a positive, he indicates. In fact, the only two people in the firm with an MBA are Afshar, who managed long/short portfolios mainly for offshore clients at Bear Stearns for 12 years, and the external chief risk officer. The firm's remaining employees have backgrounds in scientific fields, including one with experience in drug discovery, one who worked in nuclear physics, and another with expertise in particle physics.[1]

The Importance of Technology

For Afshar, the "flash crash" showed the power of technology. "The regulators should concentrate on making sure that there are no illegal market activities and allow the financial markets to find their own equilibrium," Afshar notes. It would be truly a triumph of arrogance over experience to think that the regulators can be smarter than the market. Any intervention by the regulators to maintain an orderly market in the end will do significant damage to the financial markets, capital origination, and liquidity sourcing. To those who blame high-frequency traders for the flash crash, I would ask them to read the SEC [Securities and Exchange Commission] report; the culprit was a trader who did not know how to use the computer."

For Afshar, there are several elements of technology that are important for high-frequency trading.

"One is your data feed, which has to be, depending on what kind of trading you do, extremely low latency. This includes low-latency market quotes, level 1 and level 2, and a very low-latency news feed, which is analyzed by the computer for trading. Just to give you a sense of news analytics, there are approximately 100,000 news items that come out in the United States on a typical day. The computer has to be able to read those items within less than 20 milliseconds and make a buy, sell, or hold decision; the computer identifies the novelty, relevance, and whether or not the news items are positive, negative, or neutral. This should be done within 25 milliseconds, so the latency here is nontrivial.

"Let me provide you with another example just to give you a sense of how nontrivial the latency is; if you test your data and see what would have happened if you traded about 5 seconds before you actually had the news, you would notice that the stock has in many cases started its move before the news was even time stamped; now, the movement in the stock will continue even after that, but the movement indeed started way before the news was actually out."

A low-latency data system by itself is only good if one is writing a Ph.D. thesis, Afshar claims. What is needed is to analyze those data, in Afshar's opinion, is an extremely important element, which is database management: "High-speed database management, in my opinion, is the linchpin of any computational or robotic trading system. Without a high-speed database management system, everything you do is just theoretical. To put this into perspective, a test done in Microsoft Excel that takes about five months takes five days in SQL [Structured Query Language] and less than one second in a database management system that is specifically designed for stock market and numerical analysis. This is not about having a supercomputer; this is about having database management that is very sophisticated. Of course, having low-latency data is important; having an analytics system, be it a genetic algorithm, neural network, or basic network, these are all things you cannot do without, but none of these things make any sense or has any value, monetizable value at least, if you do not have a very sophisticated high-speed database."

Afshar notes that the answer to the question of buying versus building technology has been provided rather convincingly by economists: "The answer is always to buy, except when you have quality control issues or when you have changing requirements. If you need the fastest system in the world, almost certainly you need to build it yourself. If you are not sure of all the variables and sensitivities that your model requires, it will be very hard to ask someone to provide you with an interactive system that you don't know what it is yourself."

Strategies in High-Frequency Trading

"In 2005, we had a discussion with a news wire service; they were interested in providing their machine-readable news. My first thought, having worked at Bear Sterns for a long time, was that five people can read the same news and come up with five different conclusions; even if we all read the same news and come up with the same definition that this is good news, there is no reason to be sure that the stock will necessarily go up. For example, what about when the news is good but not as good as expected, or it is as good as expected but is already reflected in the price, etc.? So I thought, this is not going to work. Now, five years later, this is actually one of the most profitable programs that we have at our shop; to think that I was one of the greatest opponents of it shows me that no amount of logic can replace evidence in financial decision making. Based on 110 million news items from several major news sources, we have been able to build a system that so far has been one of our strongest trading programs.

"High-frequency trading is becoming a commodity approach to trading. Basically, high-frequency trading is not a strategy but a means to a strategy. It is not a means to every strategy, but it is a means to basically three strategies, and only three strategies—statistical arbitrage, electronic market making, and algorithmic execution. What these three systems have in common is the fact that they are engineering approaches to investment. Engineers have a very difficult time dealing with nonlinearity; engineering students learn very early on that they should try to work the nonlinearity out of a problem. A linear example is the volume knob on the radio. As one turns the volume knob, the radio becomes louder; nonlinearity is where one turns the knob a little and the volume goes up 100-fold, and one turns the knob even more and the volume goes down. So, basically, high-frequency and low-latency trading allows the implementation of strategies that have significant amounts of engineering to capture short-term and small inefficiencies in the market. In other words, high-frequency and low-latency trading attempts to slice time slots into small enough chunks that in a particular time period the data become linear enough for the model. The same time degradation applies to the latency of price and volume quotes; it is easy to imagine that if there is significant latency in the quote delivery system, then one will have an ineffective market making operation.

"High frequency is basically an attempt to slice your information in small enough pieces that the data become linear enough for the models you are running. As the models become more sophisticated, for example, using neural network, Bayesian network, genetic algorithm, and other systems that are continuous but nonlinear, the models become more tolerant of the nonlinearity of the data. Nevertheless, I would go back to my previous point that no matter how you slice your information, the execution part of your trade is an engineering approach, and that engineering approach does require high-frequency, low-latency trading. This means that even if you are a very long-term trader, say, you are buying Coca-Cola for the next 10 years, you have to put that Coca-Cola position in place, and the execution needs to be high frequency, based on low-latency data. Then I will go one step further and say that we would need to hedge that position in Coca-Cola; even though the Coca-Cola position is very long term, the hedging is automated and again requires very high-frequency trading to continuously hedge that position."

How critical low latency is for high-frequency trading firms will depend on how sophisticated their systems and models are. The more sophisticated they are, the less sensitive they will be to latency. This does not mean that they will become immune to latency but just less sensitive, Afshar insists.

For Afshar, it is very unlikely that there will be exponential growth in market-making activities through high-frequency trading: "The growth in high-frequency trading will be controlled by the law of diminishing marginal returns, which is alive and well, even in high-frequency trading. We will reach the point of diminishing return quite quickly, given the small, although exaggerated size of the market. The growth, we believe, will be in robotic trading based on artificial intelligence, where Moore's law is also alive and well and where human discretionary intervention is at zero percent, and humans are responsible exclusively for coming up with hypotheses, identifying the data, and testing."

Finally, Afshar maintains that it is also unlikely that high-frequency trading will be as prominent as it is today when today's freshman class attends graduate school: "Given that it's nearly impossible to predict what will be the important challenges, questions, and opportunities that our world will be facing in 10 to 20 years, I would encourage them to get the best science and liberal arts education, where the emphasis is not on memorization and test preparation but on learning how to think, as John Dewey proclaimed 100 years ago."

CHAPTER 9

The Real Story Behind the "Flash Crash"

As the leader of high-frequency trading firm Tradeworx, Manoj Narang, who we will learn about a lot more about in Chapter 12, had a privileged position to observe in real time the sudden market collapse (and recovery) on May 6, 2010. He had been quoted extensively by the press even before the day of the "flash crash" as the most outspoken high-frequency trader out there. High-frequency trading was already in the public eye at that point, after a widely circulated article in the *New York Times* was published in July 2009.

According to Narang, the flash trading controversy that ensued was related to the decision on June 1, 2009, by the Nasdaq to offer Routable Flash Order and INET-Only Flash, followed by BATS on June 4, with BATS Optional Liquidity Technology (BOLT), "which consequently led to a now-infamous article in the *New York Times* on July 23 about the impact of that decision."

On June 1, when flash trading was suddenly implemented by the Nasdaq, it had quite a significant impact on high-frequency trading. Narang observed from firsthand experience that quite in contrast to what the media would have you believe, the impact that flash trading had on high-frequency trading actually was quite negative. For instance, in terms of Tradeworx's high-frequency trading strategies, Narang immediately saw a 60 percent reduction in the profitability of the company's high-frequency business. And that continued all the way through September 1, when the BATS Exchange and Nasdaq OMX Group stopped offering flash orders to their clients at the same time.

In addition, not only was the profitability of Tradeworx compromised, but Narang received many calls from colleagues in the field, wondering why their strategies suddenly stopped working.

So the other interesting aspect of this story is that there was a very intriguing and unreported reason why the Nasdaq and BATS made the decision to start using flash orders, according to Narang. The first reason was that one of their direct competitors (Direct Edge) was able to accumulate 10 percent of the market share in U.S. equities. In their opinion, that was because that exchange had a special order type called *indications of interest* that was effectively a flash order.

Furthermore, the exchanges in U.S. equities had been trying for some time to break into the rather exclusive club of options trading (dominated by a group of exchanges mostly in Chicago). The reason why the exchanges in equities had a hard time breaking into that field (which is far bigger and far more lucrative than U.S. equity trading, observes Narang) is because in order for the exchanges to start trading options, they needed high-frequency trading firms to post quotes on those options contracts. In order to do that, they required a level, open playing field, which is not what the equities field is, unfortunately, according to Narang.

Therefore, for instance, when an order is routed to an exchange in the options market (the options markets have had flash trading abilities for some time), what that means is that even if a better price is posted somewhere else, say, by a high-frequency trading firm, there is no need for the exchange to route that order out. Instead, the exchange can flash that order effectively to one of its market makers and allow that market maker to step up and fill that order.

As a result, the only trades that ever make it to the Nasdaq in options are the adversely selected orders, in other words, the orders that the market makers and the options exchanges don't want to have. This serves as a severe disincentive for high-frequency trading to post tight markets on the Nasdaq, the New York Stock Exchange (NYSE) Arca, and other equities exchanges that are trying to take market share.

The whole episode was really about the Nasdaq and BATS (to a lesser extent) trying to goad regulators to ban the practice outright on a market-wide basis, and to a small extent, they succeeded.

But much to everyone's dismay, the regulators allowed the practice to stand in the options market. So, although the experiment was unsuccessful, Narang says, it certainly has had lasting damage in terms of the public's perception of what the episode was about and what the role of high-frequency trading was.

Why High-Frequency Traders Hate Flash Orders

It's well known that some high-frequency trading firms like to earn exchange liquidity rebates as a significant percentage of their economics. This is not the case universally, says Narang, but it is the case for certain classes of strategies.

Imagine, for example, a market on which there is a 2-cent spread, say, on the Nasdaq. Let's say that there's a $19.98 bid and a $20 offer. Now suppose that a customer routes a bid-order bid to the Nasdaq to buy at $19.99. In an ordinary market, the Nasdaq would be able to post that order, and the best bid would become $19.99. However, if any other exchange were showing an offer at $19.99, then the Nasdaq's obligation under the law would be not to post that order because it would create a so-called locked market, and instead, it would be forced to route that order out to the competing exchange that is showing that $19.99 offer, thereby losing that investor's order. Thus, needless to say, exchanges are none too thrilled about having to route their orders out to competing exchanges.

So what the Nasdaq did was say that it was going to use flash orders. Instead of making that order visible, it posted it only on Nasdaq's feed. The only reason Nasdaq did this is that by not posting the order, it had not created a locked market and therefore didn't have to route that order out. In addition, the order was posted to the Nasdaq's feed for only a fraction of second.

What that did, according to Narang, was to give that order a snowball's chance of getting filled on its own exchange before it had to route it out. This is rather innocuous from Narang's perspective; in fact, it's hugely beneficial in terms of the person sending the flash order and is rather detrimental in terms of high-frequency trading. High-frequency traders would much rather have that order routed out. The reason is that the person who's very likely at that best offer at the other exchange at the price of 19.99 is very likely a high-frequency trader. And if that order were to be routed out, instead of posting at 19.99 at the other exchange, it would cross a resting offer, triggering a trade, and that would result in liquidity exchange for the person who posted the quote. The person submitting the order would be paying a market access fee of approximately 0.03 cent per share. By contrast, if that order were allowed to post via flash on the Nasdaq and then someone else were to fill the order, the person who sent the order would be entitled to a rebate because the Nasdaq posted the order. Therefore, the economic difference of those two outcomes from the perspective of the sender and the order is more than half the bid spread. It's also a significant loss for high-frequency trading of rebate income.

The flash capability of the options exchanges is the main impediment to high-frequency trading getting into the extremely lucrative business of options market making, confirms Narang. This business is dominated by heavily regulated entities with special privileges, unlike the de facto market makers in the U.S. equities markets.

The Role of the Media

According to Narang, the flash episode raised such a controversy largely because of the article printed in the *New York Times.* The paper ran an article depicting high-frequency trading as certain privileged traders trying to front-run orders from innocent retail investors. The article set off a chorus of calls for transaction taxes extensively to recoup the cost of the bailout that was precipitated by that financial crisis. Never mind the tremendous lack of logic behind such a thing, Narang implores, pointing to the implication that high-frequency trading was somehow culpable as part of Wall Street. High-frequency trading is, of course, *not* part of Wall Street. The press certainly led everyone to believe that huge banks such as Goldman Sachs and big hedge funds such as Renaissance are big players in high-frequency trading, but this is not necessarily the case. Neither of those firms is a major presence in high-frequency trading in U.S. equities, according to Narang. Indeed, the firms that had nothing to do with the credit crisis were being asked to foot the bill for the malfeasance on Wall Street. Also never mind the irony of the fact that the credit crisis was caused when the credit markets froze up because of counterparty risk.

That would never happen in an electronic exchange with central clearing, which is what high-frequency trading likes to trade on. Thus, apart from those ironies, we also got to see a whole lot of interesting political grandstanding. "If I was one of their constituents," Narang says, "I would be rather alarmed by how poorly informed congressional representatives are."

Scott Patterson, who covers high-frequency trading for the *Wall Street Journal*, explains that the emergence of high-frequency trading in the markets has received a lot of attention—and that a lot of people probably will think the attention hasn't been that great. The feedback he often gets from his articles is that the press doesn't really understand high-frequency trading very well. He would say that that is one big challenge—to get the message straight and explain exactly what is going on. He thinks that when people see that the U.S. equity markets basically have been captured by high-frequency trading (at least this is what the numbers seemed to show), it raises some alarms for people who don't understand it. The speeds freaked people out, he says.

Then people see something like the May 6 flash crash. It probably was a perfect example of how pervasive high-frequency trading has become in the market because it shows what happens when the high-frequency traders go away. Patterson has interviewed Narang in the past and has heard him saying that this was basically the greatest thing that could ever happen to high-frequency trading because it showed people that it was a necessary component of the market. This may be true, Patterson admits.

Patterson, as a reporter, gets to talk to people in all parts of the financial world to get their feedback on what is going on. Thus he speaks with a lot of high-frequency trading firms, and he also talks to institutional investors. "I can tell you that they are concerned," says Patterson. "I think part of it is because the market has evolved away from them fairly rapidly, and they are only starting to wake up to what is going on. By the way, I don't think that people are afraid that regulators are going to do something to ban this practice; that would be extremely foolish."[1]

Everyone's Worst Nightmare Coming to Fruition

Narang observes that starting with the flash controversy, all of a sudden runaway algorithms have become a major risk to the integrity of the markets, a so-called systemic risk posed by high-frequency trading. The perception of that risk has led to regulatory action such as the outlawing of sponsored access, as well as, according to Narang, all kinds of machinations that took the shape of the Securities and Exchange Commission's (SEC's) so-called concept release.

All of these misrepresentations were pretty much accepted by the high-frequency trading community as part of the bargain of doing business in a toxic environment, Narang admits. But then, without warning, on May 6, everyone's worst nightmare seemed to be coming to fruition. Narang doesn't think that it was coincidence that the media dubbed the event the "flash crash"; he thinks that it was a cynical ploy to evoke the flash controversy that precipitated the "dark age" of high-frequency trading. Now that he has had time to reflect on the so-called flash crash, it's becoming increasingly obvious that high-frequency trading played little, if any, role in what happened and that the "flash crash" itself was just another good old human panic, much like Black Monday in 1987 or the Long Term Capital Management fiasco in 1998. Neither of those was triggered by machines; they were triggered by panic selling by humans, explains Narang.

As early as May 7, 2010, it was pretty apparent to him what had happened. The markets were on hair-trigger alert because of a huge run-up (around 70 percent in 12 months) in stock prices, because of recent weakness (down around 7 percent for the week *before* May 6), and because of geopolitical events, particularly the threat that Greece and other European nations would default on their sovereign debt. Into this economic backdrop a mutual fund dumped around $4 billion worth of Standard & Poor's (S&P) E-Mini futures contracts into the open market, setting off a self-reinforcing wave of selling. Narang has calculated that the mutual fund's trade had a likely impact of about 3 percent on the S&P 500 Index's price over the course of a few minutes. This was a rather large impact, particularly at a time when the market was already spooked. Thus a snowball quickly turned into an avalanche as investors' stop-loss orders were repeatedly set off at lower and lower levels.

Ordinarily, opportunistic traders would enter the market after such a steep decline, betting on a reversal. However, the suddenness of the decline and the volume behind it made many people believe that adverse news had just come out of Europe. It was only after the Chicago Mercantile Exchange (CME) briefly halted trading that investors had a chance to find out that no news had actually hit the wire. At that point, opportunistic traders did indeed jump into the market, and the entirety of the sell-off was reversed in very short order.

Another trader close to the action was Richard Flom, vice president of trading at Systematic Alpha Management. His interpretation is that "there were some triggers on different exchanges that didn't act appropriately or acted at different times; maybe it would have made more sense to have one global trigger on all the exchanges that we could look onto further. I know that if someone was to come in and audit all the trading that happened that day, we would actually see that. We are liquidity providers. When the market goes up, we sell; when the market goes down, we buy. We have algorithms, let us say, hundreds of them, that are monitoring the market based on all kinds of strategies, time frames, and so on. So I don't think there is really any one root cause for the events and no one to blame. I do think that there are outcomes that we could learn from, though. In either case, high-frequency traders were providing liquidity when these events were happening, and the markets were dropping."[2]

Finger Pointing after the "Flash Crash"

What happened on that sleepy Thursday afternoon for the U.S. financial markets caught everybody by surprise. Jim Simons, founder of Renaissance Technologies, addressing a wealthy crowd at Tiger 21 in Manhattan, couldn't explain why people were abandoning the room during his highly awaited speech. "You can't believe what is happening in the markets now," he was told. It was totally unexpected, yet it was also highly predictable that the finger pointing would start as soon as people realized what had happened.

"I have heard a lot of rumors," says Erik Lehtis, president of DynamicFX Consulting. "Different opinions, and a lot of fingers being pointed. But I think we can all agree that the 'flash crash' was mainly due to systematic failure. At one company that I used to work for, we tried to enter inputs in the system, and the system kept rejecting them, the reason mainly being the fact that the market changed so fast that the system thought our inputs were errors. So we were unable to add liquidity to the system despite the fact that we wanted to do so. I don't think you should blame anyone for it."[3]

Lehtis thinks that fear of high-frequency trading derives from ignorance. This is probably the biggest challenge to overcome right now in terms of public opinion about the practice, he thinks, adding that high-frequency trading is not really a monolith. It encompasses a tremendous spectrum of market participants, with different agendas, different methodologies. Moreover, the participants are not all one type of firm. They can be banks, proprietary trading firms, hedge funds, and all kinds of different entities. They have different time horizons and different strategies. The only thing that they have in common is that they are using computers a lot.

High-frequency trading is being blamed for things that happened when no one really knows for sure what happened, says Lehtis. "At the same time, people are mad at high-frequency trading firms for not being in the market during the depth of the problem," he observes. "So are they the cause or are they the solution? The answer is that they are neither. With education and time, people will stop fearing high-frequency trading so much; it is just too much a part of the market."

Lehtis goes on to explain that taking the computerized automated trading out of the market will leave it with very few prices in between: "Not everybody in the market has the national interest 100 percent of the time. It is the high-frequency traders who add depth and texture to the market; they are the ones who are giving a realistic order book of liquidity on both sides of the market. And this is what everybody needs at any given point of time in order to be able to trade, so it is all about liquidity."

Peter van Kleef, CEO of Lakeview Arbitrage, offers his interpretation of what was certainly on those traders' minds back on May 6. "It is a very strange thing, I would say, that in the twenty-first century you can still have mistrades [canceled trades] in the market. If you look at the 'flash crash,' there were many trades that were canceled after the fact. I think that is one of the worst things exchanges can ever do. There's not a fixed rule in the markets for those mistrades; they can be, say, 20 percent deviation from the last price, 40 percent deviation, 50 percent deviation; the exchange is fairly free to decide what it calls a mistrade."

Narang says that his firm stayed in the market until it came close to bottoming. At that point, his traders began detecting abnormally low prices that they felt were highly likely to be retroactively "broken" by the exchanges, so they decided to exit the market. It would have been very dangerous to trade when nobody knows which of the trades actually would be allowed to stand, he explains.

"When technology is not working, when systems are screwed up, do you want the airline pilot to decide to take off, even though he or she knows the instruments are not working properly?" asks Narang. "I think the proper thing to do is to shut off. Really, the proper thing to do would have been for the exchanges to shut off, to prevent those erroneous prices from ever happening." May 6 also saw NYSE Euronext's "slow mode," which is designed to damp volatility, in action; the SEC said that the NYSE implemented its slow mode at roughly 10 times its average rate for 2010 at 2:45 p.m. that day.[4] Narang disagrees with this decision: "NYSE's decision would have been well advised if there had been market-wide protocols in place to take a time out. But, given that they weren't, the NYSE was extremely ill advised to do that."

Summarizing, Narang has three points to make. First, people can ask why high-frequency traders were not there providing liquidity, when that's their stated mandate, and people can ask why high-frequency traders turned off when volatility was sky high, given the contention that volatility benefits them. These are all valid questions, but people have to understand that strategies are not monolithic. People run different sorts of strategies.

A very common sort of strategy, statistical arbitrage, is an approach that propagates price information from stocks that are moving to stocks that haven't moved yet. It is one of the primary mechanisms for liquidity transfer in the markets. However, what this involves is propagating price information. In an environment where the inputs are wrong, propagating this information is just going to exacerbate the problem. If Procter & Gamble is down 40 percent, it is not appropriate to propagate these values to other stocks, even though they are correlated with Procter & Gamble. For those types of systems, the only responsible thing to do is to turn off because even though they serve a very valuable function in an ordinary market, which is to propagate price information, on a cross-sectional basis, they are actually counterproductive when the prices they are trying to propagate are clearly erroneous. So this is Narang's second point.

The third point, and this is perhaps the most important one, is that liquidity really should be thought of as a commodity. As such, and in any other market, it has supply and demand. Volatility is the symptom of the absence of liquidity. In May 6, there was no liquidity, so markets were free to move in huge increments in short periods of time. What's the relevance? In a supply-and-demand market, when there is a shortfall of supply or, equivalently, an excess of demand, it becomes very profitable to be a supplier in the market. When oil prices are sky-high, producers of oil make a fortune. However, that does not imply that their activity exacerbates the mismatch between supply and demand; in fact, it does the opposite. Thus, while oil producers are making money, oil prices being sky-high, by distributing oil into the marketplace, one can temper the price of oil and drive it back down by bringing the imbalance between supply and demand closer to equilibrium.

The same thing is true with liquidity, says Narang. Liquidity is the opposite of volatility. When there is volatility in the market, it is so because there is a shortfall of liquidity; there is also a shortfall of high-frequency trading because high-frequency trading is the backbone of liquidity in today's markets. For this reason, when there is volatility, it becomes extremely profitable to be a high-frequency trader. Many of the traders who continued trading on that day had very profitable trades. Tradeworx's own simulations indicated that the company would have had a record day of profits if it had kept trading. The reason the company stopped, apart from the reasons already mentioned, is that it also was concerned about the risk of broken trades.

In such circumstances, even though some firms thought they were going to earn a huge profit if they continued trading, it was not responsible to do so, unless the firm was extraordinarily capitalized and could take that risk. So this is the reason why Narang's firm turned off, not because it didn't want to be there providing liquidity. The bigger point, Narang posits, is that imbalances between supply and demand of liquidity are driven by the demand side of the equation. What Narang means by this is that on May 6, a record number of shares changed hands. So, clearly, there was a lot of high-frequency trading going on. But also clearly, it was not nearly enough to sate the demand for liquidity. This was true because liquidity shortfalls are driven by the demand side, not the supply side. As with any other supply-and-demand structure, the market cannot be assumed to be always in equilibrium. And there was no way regulators could have forced any market to be in equilibrium—that's just purely a function of supply and demand.

No matter what regulators do as part of liquidity obligations, no matter how much they force people to stay in the market, there will be times when herdlike behavior among long-term investors will see them all stampeding for the exits at the same time; there simply won't be enough high-frequency trading to cover the demand for liquidity, explains Narang. Liquidity crises are not driven by the *lack* of liquidity but by the *demand* for liquidity. This is why Narang thinks that it is a bit misguided on the part of regulators to try to prevent liquidity crises from occurring. In order to prevent liquidity crises from occurring, regulators would need to prevent herdlike behavior among long-term investors, because that's what causes bubbles and that's what causes liquidity crises.

Many factors led to the events of May 6, 2010; lots of things went wrong at the same time rather than one particular thing going wrong. Stuart Theakston of GLC, Ltd., explains, "It's now fairly well documented what occurred; a naively configured sell algorithm in the futures market, a spike in message rates, a withdrawal of high-frequency traders owing to slow/uncertain market data, a number of knock-on problems at the ECNs [electronic communications networks], and automatic marketable stop-loss orders submitted by retail clients."

John Netto, president of M3 Capital, adds: "I said that back on May 6, and I say that again, the 'flash crash' was originated from an S&P future order; there was a large block order that time of day, and at the time, there were a lot of political risks and concerns over sovereign debt in the market. And a combination of factors caused the big crash, a very precipitous fall down. More people wanted to sell, and fewer people wanted to buy, and that was what happened. In our case, no options on futures trades were canceled, and that's the benefit of it, because the price integrity is key and that is what the New York City equity market has to figure out on this side. The prices that we were trading at were real prices, and I can go out there and trade with confidence in the market on that day."

Narang has seen a palpable shift in the narrative ever since the facts have been coming out. Prior to May 6, the prevailing narrative in the press and public and circles of policymakers was that high-frequency trading induces volatility in the market when it is actually in the market trading by virtue of the sorts of strategies it runs. By contrast, after May 6, the narrative had done a 180-degree turn, saying, in effect, that high-frequency trading now causes volatility when it stops trading. This is not exactly the truth either; particularly because the majority of high-frequency trading firms did not stop trading, considering that it happened to be the second-largest volume day in history. Nevertheless, that narrative is far closer to reality than what members of the industry were confronting before that.

The second development, coming from Narang's personal experience, is that the media are starting to see that high-frequency trading is really not the province of Wall Street. High-frequency trading is way too small a business for Wall Street to care about.

The entire profits of the industry in U.S. equities are no larger than $2 to $3 billion a year, which is what a medium-sized hedge fund could make on its own in a year, says Narang. The public is not ready yet, in his mind, to come to grips with reality.

What Regulators Should Consider

After May 6, regulators were at a loss to explain what had happened and immediately set up meetings with the major exchanges to go through the events and try to come up with rules to prevent another similar event. Narang's main suggestion to regulators: "Don't bother."

He explains that they can't regulate away volatility. Volatility is an ever-present fact of markets; the only way to get rid of it is to get rid of the market itself. Regardless of the actions of regulators, such events are guaranteed to occur with regularity, he thinks. Furthermore, volatility has nothing to do with electronic trading. Historically, there has been at least one major crash every 10 years or so, regardless of which rules and regulations were in place at the time or how much technology was used by market participants.

It is especially foolish, Narang continues, to try to regulate volatility by focusing on the supply side of liquidity. All the elasticity in the market for liquidity comes from the demand side of the market, which is to say, long-term investors. Because of this, going forward, Narang expects the rate of these sorts of events to increase because capital is more concentrated and less constrained than it has ever been.

The importance of May 6 has been way overhyped, says Narang. No permanent destruction of value occurred on May 6. There was a temporary glitch lasting a couple of minutes, and it was quickly and completely reversed. As far as crashes go, this is the most innocuous one in history. The significance of this event compared with, say, the financial panic of 2008 set off by the collapse of Lehman Brothers, is the same as the significance of a mole hill sitting next to a mountain.

Agreeing with Narang, Netto suggests that regulators should follow the laissez-faire approach: "My suggestion is that in their desire to prevent a 'flash crash,' regulators shouldn't harm the structure and the character of a market that rewards people who step in and take risk and provide liquidity. And breaking trades below a certain level can disproportionately create a market environment that punishes liquidity providers. We are the most robust markets in the world; the volumes that are done in the United States from 9:30 to 11:00 a.m. make it the most intense time of the day in any 24-hour period. We have to be very careful in handling our jobs as stewards to the financial world. I would say that the regulators should follow the examples put up by the futures industry as a template to follow."

Along the same lines, Narang advises: "I would say to people who are critical about high-frequency trading: 'Get a clue.' High-frequency traders have nowhere near the capital required to create much volatility. The $4-billion-dollar trade that Waddell and Reed did, which set the 'flash crash' in motion, represents far more capital than is possessed by all high-frequency trading firms in the U.S. equity market combined!"

Narang is not the only one who is very vocal about critics of high-frequency trading. Netto is even blunter: "The critics are not actually traders, because they wouldn't make that comment if they actually were in the market."

Lehtis is not entirely against further regulation: "Although we like to think of ourselves as regulated, we are unregulated for the most part. And we would like it to stay that way. We hear a lot of talking about transaction taxes and other things that would be detrimental to high-frequency trading, so there is a huge incentive to increase volume. You add a tax to that, and you change the entire business model. I personally think that regulation is good, but we have to be very careful not to affect the process. There are certain things as far as computers and electronics are concerned that do need to be regulated. But, above all, we need to keep in mind market liquidity and transparency, which should be reserved and hopefully enhanced."

Ben Van Vliet brings a very useful analogy to bear on this subject. "Back to the NASCAR example; we all want to race fast but safe. It doesn't do any good if someone crashes into the innocent crowd and kills people. There are external people who may be affected when things crash. What we want the government to do is to create a safe track for us to race fast. And if they are going to put speed bumps in there, the racers are going somewhere else. And we won't be the center of the financial world anymore. So somebody has to create that environment. Because if the regulation is too heavy-handed and doesn't let us race fast, the volume is just going overseas. I can colocate my algorithm at any server in the world I choose. So, if you want the United States to be the world's leader in trading and where the world's capital comes to trade, you have to create fast and safe tracks for people to race."[5]

The CFTC/SEC Report

"At 2:32 p.m., a large fundamental trader (a mutual fund complex) initiated a sell program to sell a total of 75,000 E-Mini contracts (valued at approximately $4.1 billion) as a hedge to an existing equity position."[6] This is how the joint report by the staffs of the SEC and the Commodity Futures Trading Commission (CFTC) recounted the events that led on May 6 to the sell-off in which the Dow Jones Industrial Average suffered its fastest decline ever.

Regulators singled out but didn't name a Midwestern mutual fund company's computer-driven trade as the catalyst that sent a shaky market into an unprecedented tailspin. The fund had been identified by Reuters back on May 14 as Waddell & Reed Financial,

Inc.[7] "The report placed relatively little blame on the broad structure of U.S. financial markets, created and overseen by the SEC and CFTC. It didn't answer a key question: if one trade could cause so much turmoil, why hadn't that happened before?"[8]

According to the report: "This large fundamental trader chose to execute this sell program via an automated execution algorithm (sell algorithm) that was programmed to feed orders into the June 2010 E-Mini market to target an execution rate set to 9 percent of the trading volume calculated over the previous minute but without regard to price or time. The execution of this sell program resulted in the largest net change in daily position of any trader in the E-Mini since the beginning of the year (from January 1, 2010, through May 6, 2010). Only two single-day sell programs of equal or larger size—one of which was by the same large fundamental trader—were executed in the E-Mini in the 12 months prior to May 6. When executing the previous sell program, this large fundamental trader used a combination of manual trading entered over the course of a day and several automated execution algorithms that took into account price, time, and volume. On that occasion, it took more than five hours for this large trader to execute the first 75,000 contracts of the large sell program."

The report seems to absolve high-frequency traders of any responsibility for the decline; in fact, it acknowledges that some high-frequency traders remained active traders until closing; while there was a clear risk that some of the trades would be broken up, some traders took the risk and made a killing. In fact, a person with knowledge of the industry shared that a Chicago firm had made $100 million for the day. For an industry that generates $3 billion in annual profits, that was indeed a significant number for a single firm.

According to Lebovitz, "What the report missed was that the liquidity trap that day was closely tied to global economic conditions, there was tremendous fear about the state of European banks and even the stability of some governments, and risk appetites diminished significantly in the days leading up to May 6. In our case, we traded uninterrupted in most markets throughout the entire day. None of our trades were canceled. I'm quite comfortable saying that our activity did nothing to accelerate or exacerbate the volatility that day."

Just a few days later, David Cummings, chairman of Tradebot Systems, Inc., sent around the perfect autopsy of the "flash crash," an e-mail entitled, "Waddell Stupidity Caused Crash" about Waddell & Reed, the company whose E-Mini futures trade conspired with the perfect storm to cause the events of May 6:

> Wow! Who puts in a $4.1 billion order without a limit price? The trader at Waddell & Reed showed historic incompetence. However, on May 6, when markets were already under stress, the sell algorithm chosen by the large trader and set to target only trading volume, and neither price nor time, executed the sell program extremely rapidly in just 20 minutes. The execution of this sell program resulted in the largest net change in daily position of any trader in E-Minis since the beginning of the year. This was a human mistake. The trader easily could have put a price limit on the order but recklessly chose not to. The sell algorithm performed exactly as it was designed. It angers me when people blame technology for what are clearly lapses in human judgment. Now that the regulators know what happened, what are they going to do? Is there any penalty for massively disrupting the market? Are we going to let people throw around billion-dollar orders with no understanding of market impact? After the "flash crash" but before the CFTC/SEC report came out, Waddell executives were unloading stock in their company. Maybe these brilliant market timers expect things to get worse.[9]

CHAPTER 10

Meet the Speed Traders: Stuart Theakston

"High-frequency trading is really about using mathematical models in computer programs to monitor and trade thousands of securities at a time. If you look, you can see that we are buying a share for 10.25 and then we're selling it one second later at 10.26. So that is fairly high frequency for a one-penny profit."

This is how Stuart Theakston explained high-frequency trading to BBC presenter Paul Lewis for *Money Box*. Theakston is the head of quantitative research and automated trading at GLC, Ltd., managing all research and development for the quantitative models and trading systems. (GLC is an acronym of its founders' first names, Gilbert Hall, Lawrence Staden and Caroline Moxon.) He started with the firm in 2008, heading the high-frequency trading desk. Prior to GLC, Ltd., Theakston founded a quantitative proprietary trading business deploying equity long/short strategies. He also has worked at Merrill Lynch and Deutsche Bank, with responsibility for delivering quantitative trading tools and high-performance execution products to hedge fund clients and internal trading desks.

"I am a finance and technology junkie, so that is my work motivation. Success to me is building systems—in the widest possible sense: software, teams, trading strategies—that generate substantial wealth."

Early Interest and Professional Beginnings

"I got the tech bug early, like many British kids of my generation; my first computer was a Sinclair ZX81 (with a massive 1 K of memory) that I got at the age of 10. I did a lot of programming; everyone did, because there was no other way to use computers then. It is actually a shame that now kids use them without having any idea how they actually work."

Theakston became interested in financial markets at about that time. His parents bought him some shares in Acorn Computers (from which ARM was later spun out) at about the age of 10. Acorn was a local company near Cambridge, England. Theakston used to go to the school library every day to look up the share price in the newspaper. At age 14, he started actively trading in the stock market. By a quirk of the settlement system used at the time on the London Stock Exchange (all trades in a fixed two-week period settled on the same day after the end of the period), it was possible to trade large positions with no money whatsoever and go short without having to borrow shares, as long as positions were closed out in the two-week account period. And this was exactly what he did.

"I used to be regularly late for class because I was on the pay phone waiting for a broker to give me a fill. I missed most of the school day on the afternoon of 19 October 1987 because I was in a local television shop watching the Black Monday unfold on TELETEXT, which was the closest you could get to real-time prices as a retail trader in 1987. It was impossible to get through to any stockbrokers on the phone that day, an early lesson in who is able to access markets at times of stress."

After school, Theakston obtained an honors degree in computer science from Cambridge University. He had a fantastic time there and made many lifelong friends; for him, it was an incredibly stimulating atmosphere, not just educationally but socially and politically too. On graduation, he joined Goldman Sachs in London on its graduate trainee program. The week he joined Goldman, late 1994, at the tail end of a bear bond market, Goldman made a significant number of redundancies globally and canceled his training program (he was supposed to have spent eight weeks in New York). He was put straight to work in technology development on the stock lending desk on the equities trading floor. Goldman was still a partnership at the time and had only about a thousand employees in London; Theakston didn't fully appreciate this at the time, but he thinks it was a great atmosphere, the proactive "can-do" attitude was amazing, the openness to new ideas, and lack of fighting between business units; all was in stark contrast to what he would experience later at other investment banks.

"I went from Goldman to Deutsche Bank in the late nineties to manage equity finance technology (securities lending, repo, and the like); the bank was building an investment bank by buying in talent, which included the head of my desk at Goldman; he made me an offer I couldn't refuse to move to Deutsche Bank. I had made the mistake of thinking that all investment banks were like Goldman Sachs, and I couldn't have been more wrong. At that time, Deutsche Bank was a snake pit of feudal infighting. With hindsight, this is inevitable if you build an investment bank by buying in talent: It's going to attract the most mercenary people by construction. After a stint in venture capital in 2000–2002 as cofounder and CTO of Armada Partners, a Deutsche Bank–sponsored Internet business incubator, I returned to Deutsche Bank to help build out its direct market access (DMA) and algorithmic trading products. It was there that I started working with hedge funds to help them implement systematic quantitative and high-frequency strategies. I joined GLC, Ltd., in January 2008 as head of research and am now head of quantitative research and automated trading (which encompasses high-frequency trading)."

The Impact of High-Frequency Trading

In the broadest view, Theakston says, high-frequency trading is any sort of trading where trade decisions are made, and orders managed, by a computer, and positions are held for less than a day; he admits that some people would consider it market microstructure arbitrage only, and others would say that it is not high frequency nowadays unless your time to market is in microseconds and you burn your algorithms directly into silicon for maximum performance. Nevertheless, he would stick with the broadest view.

"I think on balance the impact of high-frequency traders is a positive one, for all other market participants (except for other high-frequency traders!). Ignoring for a minute the minutiae of the debate about market stability (e.g., 'flash crash'), for the most part, high-frequency traders are competing to provide liquidity. This is particularly good for retail investors because they are likely to trade aggressively (in the order-book sense) in small size and so have fewer concerns about activities such as order anticipation that tend to (probably wrongly) upset institutional investors. Your suppliers competing furiously with one another is never a bad thing.

"High-frequency traders simply replace specialists/jobbers in providing liquidity in a much more competitive framework. Liquid and efficient markets are important for economic development. I do have some sympathy with those who feel that high-frequency traders spending millions of dollars on infrastructure to be a few microseconds faster than the other guy is somehow, from a social perspective, not money 'well spent.' However, this is just the way that competitive markets find equilibrium."

What Makes High-Frequency Trading Controversial

Theakston clearly has spent a lot of time thinking about the reputation of high-frequency trading in the financial world. He has a gift for succinctly analyzing and summing up the situation. Everyone loves to have a scapegoat, he says, and high-frequency trading has all the attributes required to make a perfect scapegoat:

- It is hard to understand, or at least it takes a bit of effort to understand (even professional long-only institutional investors have difficulty understanding it).
- It is fairly exclusive. The firms involved either have no incentive to talk about what they do (because they are proprietary trading firms and don't need to attract external capital) or are not allowed to (because they are hedge funds and have regulatory constraints on marketing themselves). Its exclusivity is enhanced by most of the individual participants having very high levels of academic qualifications, mostly Ph.D.s.
- It has some large dollar numbers associated with it (although more in terms of turnover than profitability).
- It has lots of terminology associated with it that sounds geeky and confusing to the uninitiated: "microsecond," "colocate," "momentum ignition," "quote stuffing," "temporal arbitrage," etc.
- Some intelligent, well-informed, and eminently quotable people are railing against it, including Paul Wilmott and Richard Bookstaber, among others. Wilmott, editor of his own journal of quantitative finance, rails against high-frequency traders who try to guess what the price will do over the next few milliseconds, arguing that the industry should be concerned with what the value is.
- It is prone to occasionally be a contributory factor (or, in fact, its switching off is a contributory factor) to events perceivable by the public, such as the so-called flash crash.

The May 6, 2010 "flash crash" indeed exposed a number of misconceptions about the industry, the biggest one being the claim that high-frequency traders were somehow "taking advantage" of other investors. For Theakston, that is entirely bogus, because high-frequency traders are actually getting paid, in a very competitive market, to provide a service to other investors (that service is immediate liquidity). He thinks that the media and the public don't realize that this is a competitive situation where abnormal risk-adjusted returns are being competed away by a large number of market participants. The media fail to understand this in pretty much every context because the "greedy company taking advantage of innocent consumers" story is all too common, he says.

"They also fail to understand the amount of intellectual and technology infrastructure required to engage in high-frequency trading and so think that high-frequency traders are getting a 'free lunch.' In actual fact, they are just eating each other's lunches in an ultracompetitive frenzy that ends with a large number of them being unable to cover their fixed costs and going out of business, leaving a few very competitive outfits making only normal profits. This is how competitive markets are supposed to work and is what institutional/retail investors should want.

"There are obviously risks that overzealous regulators will kill the industry; the most extreme example would be something like a Tobin tax, which would take the liquidity landscape for most assets back to the 1960s. Politically motivated tinkering is more likely to take the form of a measure such as minimum rest times for orders (where you have to leave orders out for at least a second, for example), but inevitably, these sorts of rules will be implemented on a country-by-country basis, so high-frequency traders will just choose to provide their liquidity wherever the rules are sensible. Regulatory environments with a more laissez-faire attitude to high-frequency traders will enjoy more liquid markets as a result.

"The whole high-frequency trading controversy is a complete red herring; there is no fundamental problem at all. My suggestion for regulators is: do nothing. I don't think any regulatory change is required at all. Market structures are evolving things, and early in their evolution there will be problems. The obligated liquidity provision of the specialist system evolved over more than 100 years into a very robust but ultimately slow and expensive system. The system that replaced it, a free-for-all of competing exchanges and high-frequency traders, has been in existence a little over half a decade. Every incident such as the so-called flash crash merely strengthens the market structure by changing the participants' behavior; it is to some extent self-healing. For example, looking at the 'flash crash,' in order to avoid getting burned again, retail traders now will put limit prices on their stop-loss orders, ECNs [electronic communications networks] will be quicker to cut off on-routing to other venues they suspect of having issues, and people will make sure that their futures algorithmic orders are configured properly because if they don't, they will lose money, and it will get taken away from them and given to participants who are more careful. This is the mechanism by which competitive markets lead to stronger, fairer systems.

"As an aside, some of the actions of the exchanges and regulators on the day of the 'flash crash' actually have made the situation worse for the future by introducing a moral hazard. By retrospectively busting some trades, they have incentivized high-frequency traders and other participants *not* to provide liquidity when it is most needed because, by doing so, they run the risk of getting one leg of a trade busted and causing them to be left with the residual, probably loss-making positions. This was a typical knee-jerk reaction. The best thing that the exchanges and ECNs could have done to ensure that this sort of thing didn't happen again was to let all the trades stand. This would have rewarded, rather than punished, those who stepped into the breach and provided liquidity when it was most needed.

"Having said all that, I think that there is no harm in implementing some sort of version of the European-style volatility suspensions as long as they don't assume that some venue is the 'primary' venue and embed their incumbent advantage in the rule book."

The Risks of High-Frequency Trading

Theakston would like to say that there are no risks involved with the increasing popularity of high-frequency trading, yet it is not quite that simple, he admits. First, "I'd argue with the premise that there is exponential growth in high-frequency trading. I think it is starting to slow down of its own accord because the alpha increasingly is being competed away, and the infrastructure investment required to be faster than your competitors carries increasingly diminishing returns. This will reach a natural competitive equilibrium, and I don't think we are that far from that point. We do need to see some people withdrawing from the business to be sure we are there."

"I don't think anything 'needs to be done' to avoid these risks. I think we just need to allow competitive markets to take their course. Neither exchanges nor high-frequency traders are monopoly providers anymore, so the competitive dynamic should be sufficient to achieve stability without regulatory intervention. Why? Here are some examples:

- "If I run an exchange/ECN/MTF [multilateral trading facility] and one of my customers 'quote-stuffs' me to slow down my systems to try to gain an unfair edge, I can simply kick that customer off my system. If I don't, then other users will not want to trade on my platform, and I will go out of business. Therefore, no regulation is required.

- "A high-frequency trader tries to take advantage of other investors by using momentum ignition strategies. In a competitive market, any short-term deviation from fundamental value will be competed away by other market participants—in this case, high-frequency traders with a mean reversion bias. Long-only institutional investors particularly don't like this sort of behavior. But, as an institutional investor, I am as likely to be able to take advantage of this (say, by selling into an upward spike) as I am to be disadvantaged by it. It is just that human nature causes me to blame someone else for the trades that go against me and take credit for the trades that work out. This is why they complain about it.
- "High-frequency traders switch off when the markets go haywire, exaggerating any sudden moves, because they are fair-weather market makers with no obligation to provide liquidity. This is actually a problem of perception and mental accounting. Under the old specialist (U.S.)/jobber (U.K.) system, there was a market-making obligation, so you didn't have 'flash crashes.' But the cost of handing these guys a monopoly was enormous. One went maybe five years paying much higher spreads to avoid one day of bad intraday mark-to-market losses. Because the costs are concentrated (the 'flash crash') and the benefits dispersed, people make a mental accounting error in thinking that the costs outweigh the benefits, whereas, in fact, they don't; they are just distributed differently. As an aside, there is a similar mental accounting error that causes people to object to free trade: the benefits are dispersed (slightly cheaper goods for everyone), and the costs are concentrated (some people lose their jobs). Even though the dispersed benefits are greater than the concen-

trated costs, people still perceive it as a net negative, even though it is not."

High-Frequency Trading Strategies

For Theakston, the most profitable high-frequency trading strategies are obviously the ones nobody talks about, but there's a real question about how one defines *profitable.*

"There is a contention between Sharpe ratio and capacity (all high-frequency strategies are very capacity constrained), so what is 'most profitable' rather depends on your circumstances, that is:

- "How much capital have you got?
- "What infrastructure do you already have?
- "How big a drawdown can you handle in the event of a system or market failure?
- "Are you running your own (proprietary) capital or client money?

"The size of the after-costs opportunity set for high-frequency trading of any kind is not as large as the media seem to think it is. Addressing the ongoing examination of high-frequency trading practices in financial markets, researchers Michael Kearns, Alex Kulesza, and Yuriy Nevmyvaka, from the Computer and Information Science Department at the University of Pennsylvania, published 'Empirical Limitations on High-Frequency Trading Profitability'[1] in September 2010, in which they reported the results of an extensive empirical study estimating the maximum possible profitability of the most aggressive such practices and arrived at a figure that was surprisingly modest, $3.4 billion, a figure any individual person or trading group would be happy to reap but perhaps small considering their initial assumptions."

GLC, Ltd., and High-Frequency Trading

Theakston is head of quantitative research and automated trading at GLC, Ltd., is an independent alternative asset manager based in London. Established in 1992, GLC, Ltd., focuses on various absolute return strategies—equity statistical arbitrage, short- and midterm CTAs (commodity trading advisors), and discretionary macro. Today, the company manages more than $1 billion in assets from a global institutional investor base and has more than 55 employees. GLC, Ltd., invests in a range of asset classes, including equities, fixed income, foreign exchange, and commodities and their derivative instruments. Investors have access to a range of single and multistrategy funds. GLC, Ltd. provides six different commingled funds and managed accounts tailored to institutional clients.

"I spend perhaps 70 percent of my time with our team of quants, traders, and programmers and 30 percent of my time watching the markets and doing research myself. I have a long commute and read a lot of academic papers, journals, etc. on the train. I do nothing but work and sleep during the week. On the weekends, I try to spend as much time with my two young children as possible; this doesn't really leave much time for anything else.

"Our firm is a very entrepreneurial and innovative environment; we try to make it an exciting and stimulating environment in which to work, as well as a materially rewarding one. For us to start high-frequency trading, for example, it took us, literally, two guys, a load of computers, and preexisting institutional access to markets, with the overlay of an existing operational and risk-management architecture. We now trade high-frequency strategies in equities across all liquid European markets, as a small part of our equity statistical arbitrage program. Increasingly, we are using the tools we have built in high frequency to better manage our order flow for the rest of the program. This is a fairly well-trodden path for those using these techniques in a client money environment owing to the intrinsically capacity-constrained nature of 'pure' high-frequency trading.

"We constantly improve our technology by having a small team of developers who sit on the desk and work very closely with the traders and risk managers. Some roles are hybrid technology/trading roles. This has worked very well for an organization our size. We try to focus our development energies where we have that edge and buy/use open-source solutions where we have none. The key to the buy/build decision is as much about understanding where your competitive edge isn't as where it is."

In terms of infrastructure, low latency is important, but just how important depends on the strategy, says Theakston. Order-anticipation strategies and cross-venue arbitrage are obviously ultrasensitive to latency; microstructure liquidity provision is less so. The strategies Theakston runs are liquidity-providing in nature, so they are less sensitive to latency than some of the more aggressive proprietary trading businesses. Market data vendors, brokers, and colocation firms have an incentive to play up how important latency is, he says, so that they can sell the latest technology at great expense.

For Theakston, visibility of the order flow and institutional orders is very important, too. Most true high-frequency trading is microstructure and temporal arbitrage and is driven pretty much exclusively by the visibility of orders and executions; without it, there is not much to drive the models.

The dynamics of high-frequency trading mean that different approaches are open to different participants because of their cost/revenue structure.

"Proprietary trading firms can spend 99 cents on infrastructure to make one dollar; those trading client money can only spend, say, 19 cents, assuming that they are on a classical '2 and 20' [typical management fee for hedge funds, 2 percent of the fund's net asset value each year and performance fee of 20 percent of the fund's profit] fee scheme; this means that these participants cannot compete in the same space. Those trading with client money may focus on strategies that require more capital per unit of infrastructure expense, whereas for proprietary trading firms it is the opposite."

The Future of High-Frequency Trading

Theakston considers that the industry is nearing the bottom in terms of competition to be the fastest, and a once-handful of players are colocated in the exchanges' racks, all linked to other venues by direct fiber, and they run their trading agents in silicon or on graphics processing units (GPUs). Execution is only going to get faster at a Moore's law–type rate.

"There's probably a bit more evolution in terms of getting your trading agent into the CPU core next to the CPU core that's running the exchange's order book, but you can't really get any closer than that. I think the next areas of concentration for high-frequency traders are likely to be different asset classes such as foreign exchange, exchange-traded credit default swaps (CDS), and developing markets.

"I don't see more traditional investment managers expanding into high-frequency trading. There are already too many participants with too much money chasing the finite alpha available in the pure high-frequency space. But what is considered high frequency will change. Traditional investment managers are already using more and more algorithmic tools, either their own or their brokers, to execute their business. These tools will become more latency-aware and so may start to look very much like what we consider high-frequency trading today.

"I don't think retail investors will be able to run high-frequency trading strategies either. I hate to be elitist about it, but why would they? Is that really a good use of their time? I would say not. It is an enormously complex undertaking that requires a deeply specialist understanding of market microstructure, finance, and technology. There is also only finite alpha in the opportunity set, and it is very hard to argue that retail investors have any 'edge' that will enable them to beat the professionals to it. Depressingly inevitable, suppliers will spring up who try to sell 'high-frequency trading in a box' to the masses, but equally inevitably, those retail users won't make any money, at least on a properly risk-adjusted basis. As an aside, this retail disadvantage does not apply across the entire money-management business. Retail investors do have some advantages over institutions—specifically their ability to ignore monthly, quarterly, and annual performance measurements—but this gives no advantage in high frequency, where there is no 'long-term' investment."

For Theakston, most of the development in high-frequency trading has been in developed-market equity and equity derivative markets, and these are approaching maturity. These markets are likely to be the domain of increasingly specialist outfits. The low-hanging fruit has been picked. The next wave, he thinks, is likely to be in emerging markets and in other, esoteric exchange-traded products; this is where people developing their careers in this space should focus, he concludes.

CHAPTER 11

Life After the "Flash Crash"

After May 6, 2010, an abundance of unanswered questions remained as the entire financial world sought to find a reasonable explanation for the events that befell the market. Who or what was the culprit? Why did markets spin out of control so rapidly? What needed to be done to prevent this type of event from happening again? The Securities and Exchange Commission (SEC) and the Commodity Futures Trading Commission (CFTC) said they were examining the cause of the unusual trading activity. Mary L. Schapiro, chairwoman of the SEC, and Gary Gensler, head of the CFTC, held conference calls with overseers of the exchanges who were reviewing trading tapes from the day.

One official said that he identified "a huge, anomalous, unexplained surge in selling" at about 2:45 p.m. The source remained unknown, but that jolt apparently set off trading based on computer algorithms, which, in turn, rippled across indexes and spiraled out of control. It would be only a week later that Reuters identified the mutual fund complex that triggered the selloff.

Initial Speculation, May 2010

Was it a software glitch? A hacker's attack? A foreign power? A Citi trader entering an erroneous order? These suspicions and rumors, along with many others, spread out quickly on May 6. Only days later, the market was slowly able to catch a glimpse of what and who were behind the "flash crash."

May 12, 2010

"High-frequency trading doesn't benefit the financial system and should be taxed to raise money for the Securities and Exchange Commission," said Mario Gabelli, chairman and CEO of Gamco Investors, Inc., on this date. "Is the net benefit of having this extra liquidity worth it to the system? The answer is no," Gabelli said in an interview on Bloomberg Television. "Should we put a tax on this fast trading to raise revenues for the SEC? The answer is yes, so that investors benefit, not traders."

He complained that the flash traders, the dark pools, and other traders were taking over the investment process and, at the margin, becoming too important. He said that the best way investors can protect themselves from market turmoil was to examine the intrinsic value of an enterprise, which doesn't change minute by minute the way commodities change, and look through the daily volatility.[1]

May 14, 2010

The big mystery seller of futures contracts during the market meltdown on May 6 had not been a hedge fund or a high-frequency trader, as many had suspected, but money manager

Waddell & Reed Financial, Inc., according to a document obtained by Reuters.

The firm on May 6 sold a large order of E-Mini contracts during a 20-minute span in which U.S. equities markets plunged, briefly wiping out nearly $1 trillion in market capital, an internal document from Chicago Mercantile Exchange parent CME Group, Inc., said on this date. The E-Minis are one of the most liquid futures contracts in the world, providing holders exposure to the benchmark Standard & Poor's 500 Index. The contracts can act as a directional indicator for the underlying stock index. Regulators and exchange officials quickly focused on Waddell's sale of 75,000 E-Mini contracts, which the document said "superficially appeared to be anomalous activity."

Waddell managed the $22.1 billion Ivy Asset Strategy fund, which was well known for hedging with equity index futures when manager Mike Avery, who was also chief investment officer at the company, felt uneasy about the market. Back then, it was still unclear what impact the trading in the E-Minis had on stock prices during the plunge, but regulators had scrutinized futures trading because the sharp decline in that market preceded the dive in the broader U.S. equities market. The document said that during the sell-off and subsequent rally, other active traders in E-Minis included Jump Trading, Goldman Sachs Group, Inc., Interactive Brokers Group, Inc., JPMorgan Chase & Co., and Citadel Group.

Kansas-based Waddell had declined to return calls seeking comment. In a statement, however, the company said, "Like many market participants, Waddell & Reed was affected negatively by the market activity of May 6." Waddell said in its statement that it often uses futures trading to "protect fund investors from downside risk," and on May 6, it executed several trading strategies, including the use of index futures contracts as part of normal operations.[2] Of course, the new normal also included

Waddell insiders selling their shares, in anticipation of the scrutiny they were sure to face in the coming months.

May 24, 2010

The SEC and the CFTC hosted their first meeting of the Joint CFTC-SEC Advisory Committee on Emerging Regulatory Issues, which discussed the preliminary findings of the staffs of the CFTC and SEC related to the unusual market events of May 6.[3] As a result, the SEC was moving closer to eliminating traders' use of *stub quotes*, placeholder prices that tend to be far from an actual market price. Presenting their preliminary findings of the May 6 market plunge, SEC staffers had said that they found "virtually no defenders" of stub quotes in their talks with the trading exchanges and other market participants. Stub quotes were used by firms when they didn't want to trade; when a firm wanted to pull away and ensured that no trades occurred, it offered quotes that were wildly out of bounds, such as an offer to buy for one penny a share or sell for $100,000. Normally, such trades wouldn't get executed. But investigators of the "flash crash" believed that some trades were suddenly executed unintentionally at stub-quote prices during the afternoon of May 6, when the market inexplicably dropped and recovered.[4]

May 26, 2010

Manoj Narang, who we will learn about in detail in Chapter 12, explained to attendees to a leading industry conference his version of the facts that led to the dramatic swing in the Dow Jones on May 6. He also explained why his firm didn't think it would have been responsible to continue trading that day: "Everyone who has been paying attention the past few months to our space probably recognizes that the industry has been mired in a bit of a 'dark age.' This period is bookended by sentences that have the word 'flash' in them, for instance, the great flash controversy about the 'flash crash' that we just experienced on May 6."[5]

May 26, 2010

On this date, Goldman Sachs Group, Inc. announced that it would offer clients direct market access and algorithmic trading for Brazilian stocks as competition builds for market share in Latin America's biggest bourse. Goldman Sachs' clients would be able to trade electronically through the bank's local subsidiary, the firm said in a statement. UBS AG, Switzerland's biggest bank, and Bank of America Corp., the biggest U.S. lender, had begun offering the trading the year before. Algorithmic, or high-frequency, trading uses computers to analyze market conditions to determine how much of a stock or derivative to buy and when.

Bruno Carvalho, Goldman Sachs' head of futures and electronic trading for Latin America, said in a statement that the company saw significant opportunities in Brazil, particularly because international interest and capital inflows into the country continued to increase.[6] Goldman was not the only one; Brazil (together with India, Russia, and China) was always mentioned as the next expansion geography for high-frequency trading.

Thorough Investigation, June–September 2010

As more details about the events of May 6 emerged, some high-frequency traders welcomed the closer scrutiny. "We are not a no-regulation crowd," said Richard Gorelick, cofounder of the high-frequency trading firm RGM Advisors in Austin, Texas. "We were all created by good regulation, the regulation that provided for more competition, more transparency, and more fairness."[7] Indeed, the decimalization, Regulation ATS, and Regulation NMS, all initiatives championed by the regulators, had been catalysts for development of the high-frequency trading industry; furthermore, Arthur Levitt, former chairman of the SEC who spearheaded many of these initiatives, had become advisor to GETCO.

June 2, 2010

On this date, the SEC hosted a public forum to examine securities market structure issues. The roundtable featured in-depth discussions of key market structure issues, including high-frequency trading, undisplayed liquidity, and the appropriate metrics for evaluating market structure performance. Panelists included representatives of retail and institutional investors, issuers, exchanges, alternative trading systems (ATSs), financial services firms, high-frequency traders, and the academic community. The high-frequency trading community was represented by Richard Gorelick, CEO of RGM Advisors, and Stephen Schuler, CEO of GETCO.[8]

June 4, 2010

On this date, Singapore Exchange Limited (SGX) announced that it was investing $250 million in a new initiative to boost trading speeds and enhance connectivity with global financial markets. This consisted of $70 million for a new securities-trading engine and $180 million for infrastructure outsourcing services and data centers, collectively known as the *Reach initiative.* The initiative, aimed at bolstering liquidity and high-frequency trading, would be rolled out from the first quarter of 2011. Migration of the securities-trading engine would start in 2011, followed by derivatives trading, which was expected to take place in about two years' time.

High-frequency trading already accounted for about 30 percent of derivatives trading on Singapore's exchange but was not significant yet in equities trading. The new trading engine, SGX Reach, would provide the lowest end-to-end latency in the world. It was delivered through Nasdaq OMX's Genium platform, Voltaire's InfiniBand solution, and Hewlett-Packard's (HP's) technology. On May 7, SGX had conducted a benchmark test with partners at HP's Singapore Capacity Planning Centre and established an average order response time of 90 microseconds door to door, the fastest in the world and over 100 times faster than SGX's current Quest-ST system. Prior to this, the fastest trading system was run by the Nasdaq and took 177 microseconds to execute trades.

Customers who colocated at this data center could transact with SGX's trading engine at the lowest possible latency for a monthly colocation fee. About 40 percent of SGX's brokering members had already signed up as the first batch of subscribers.

The Reach initiative also included establishing presence at key data centers in Chicago, London, New York, and Tokyo. SGX said that this would allow customers in these places to connect directly with SGX's trading engine at lower cost and facilitate participation in Asia's growing markets by a larger number of global trading firms. The network of these SGX hubs may be expanded in the future to other financial centers, including Hong Kong.[9]

June 9, 2010

Matthew Andresen, former president of electronic stock market operator Island ECN, bought by Instinet Group, and cohead of the Citadel group that made markets in stocks and equity derivatives, and Jason Lehman, who ran Citadel's global options business, disclosed that they were co-CEOs of the newly formed Headlands Technologies, LLC. Joining them was former colleague Neil Fitzpatrick, who had been operations chief of Citadel's unit specializing in global equities trading and options order routing. The startup trading company was reuniting top managers from a division of Citadel that during the men's time working there grew into a big moneymaker for the firm.

Citadel Execution Services, as the trading and market-making unit was called, was separate from the asset-management business for which Citadel was better known. The firm until recently went by the name Citadel Investment Group but had shortened that to one word. Asset management was the arm through which pension funds and other investors placed money in Citadel's hedge funds.

Profits in the separate trading unit had helped Citadel to weather rare steep losses in its hedge funds in 2008, when the credit crisis battered many investment funds. During that period, Citadel Execution Services flourished, as did Citadel's business making markets for options. Within the same division, Citadel's high-frequency trading operation brought in about $1 billion that year, reflecting Citadel's expanding influence in the fast-growing world of computer-powered trading.

The Headlands partners had secured outside funding from firms such as the Tudor Investment Corporation to help start the firm and planned to invest the firm's money through the new quantitative trading operation, Andresen said. The investment focus was still evolving, but it might include trading in stocks, options, and futures markets across a variety of geographies, he said.[10]

June 10, 2010

On this date, the SEC approved rules that require the exchanges and the Financial Industry Regulatory Authority (FINRA) to pause trading in certain individual stocks if the price moves 10 percent or more in a five-minute period. The rules, which were proposed by the national securities exchanges and FINRA and published for public comment, came in response to the market disruption of May 6.

"The May 6 market disruption illustrated a sudden, but temporary, breakdown in the market's price-setting function when a number of stocks and ETFs [exchange-traded funds] were executed at clearly irrational prices," said SEC chairwoman Mary L. Schapiro, who convened a meeting of the exchange leaders and FINRA at the SEC following the market disruption. She added that by establishing a set of circuit breakers that uniformly pause trading in a given security across all venues, these new rules would ensure that all markets pause simultaneously and provide time for buyers and sellers to trade at rational prices. Under the rules, trading in a stock would pause across U.S. equity markets for a five-minute period in the event that the stock experienced a 10 percent change in price over the preceding five minutes. The pause, which would apply to stocks in the Standard & Poor's (S&P) 500 Index, would give the markets the opportunity to attract new trading interest in an affected stock, establish a reasonable market price, and resume trading in a fair and orderly fashion.

Initially, these new rules would be in effect on a pilot basis through December 10, 2010. Listening to requests from the New York Stock Exchange (NYSE), Nasdaq, Direct Edge, and BATS, the SEC later would extend these new rules for four more months while the exchange, other national securities exchanges, and the commission would further assess the effect of the pilot on the marketplace or whether other initiatives should be adopted in lieu of the pilot.[11] "It is my hope to rapidly expand the program to thousands of additional publicly traded companies," added Chairwoman Schapiro.[12]

June 11, 2010

On this date, GETCO hired Elizabeth King, associate director of the SEC's trading and markets division, as the SEC stepped up scrutiny of the fragmented, mostly electronic marketplace and considered new rules to ensure fair access to public markets. King's former division was responsible for crafting controversial proposals to rein in short sellers, or investors who profit on a stock's decline, as well as proposals to ban the so-called flash orders that caused a stir in the preceding year and helped spark a wide-ranging review of the U.S. market structure. She would join GETCO's legal unit and probably be instrumental in helping the Chicago-based company navigate regulatory issues with the SEC.[13]

The move prompted Senator Charles Grassley from Iowa to fire a letter to the SEC just three days later, sharing his concern about regulators taking jobs at the very companies they have been regulating in a practice known as the *revolving door*. In response, the SEC's inspector general opened a probe into the former high-ranking staffer's move.[14]

Not content with only strengthening its U.S. compliance team, GETCO four months later would hire Jennifer Boneham, a senior staffer at the U.K.'s Financial Services Authority (FSA), in the latest sign that the firm was tapping talent at regulators and rival businesses as it grew its business. Boneham was in the markets infrastructure and policy unit of the FSA, run by David Lawton, ultimately reporting to Alexander Justham, head of markets and capital markets.[15]

June 22, 2010

The Joint CFTC-SEC Advisory Committee on Emerging Regulatory Issues held its second public meeting on this date because it was conducting a review of the unusual market events that occurred on May 6, 2010. The committee heard from representatives of exchanges and significant market participants about their views and observations relating to market events of that day. SEC chairwoman Mary L. Schapiro and CFTC chairman Gary Gensler were the cochairs of the committee. The high-frequency trading community was represented by David Cummings, owner and chairman of the board of Tradebot Systems; Anoop Prasad, managing director of D. E. Shaw and Co.; and Matt Schrecengost, COO of Jump Trading, LLC.[16]

June 25, 2010

On this date, GETCO announced the European launch of GETCO Execution Services (GES). The GES trading platform provided investors with direct and anonymous access to the dedicated liquidity of GETCO's market-making division. Importantly, GES promised to reduce systemic risk by ensuring central counterparty clearing for all participants, the first trading venue of its kind in Europe to do so. GES's liquidity was made possible by GETCO's position as a leading market maker on more than 50 exchanges, electronic communications networks (ECNs), ATSs, and multilateral trading facilities (MTFs) in North and South America, Europe, and Asia.[17]

July 21, 2010

On this date, Direct Edge announced the operational launch of its EDGA and EDGX exchange platforms and the commencement of trading across all listed stock symbols. Direct Edge had received exchange approval from the SEC in March 2010 and begun the process of transitioning from its legacy ECN platforms to its next-generation exchange-trading systems.[18] Direct Edge was locating its new platforms, EDGA handling the higher-performance needs of proactive black-box statistical arbitrage and active algorithmic traders and EDGX focused more on passive black-box and agency algorithmic trading, at Equinix's NY4 data center in Secaucus, New Jersey, with a backup facility operated by Telx in Clifton, New Jersey.[19]

It was a remarkable turn of events for the firm that had begun operations in 1998 as Attain ECN. In 2005, it had been purchased by Knight Capital Group, rebranded, and introduced as Direct Edge ECN. In 2007, Knight spun off Direct Edge as an independent company, bringing on Citadel Securities and Goldman Sachs as partners. Direct Edge eventually would trade 2 billion shares each day and account for about 12 percent of trading in U.S. equities.

August 11, 2010

On this date, Senator Charles Schumer from New York called on regulators to clarify the role of the market-making firms that were supposed to maintain liquidity and to legally bind some high-frequency traders to provide liquidity to U.S. stock markets as part of an effort to prevent a repeat of the May 6 "flash crash." Senator Schumer was reacting to an SEC investigation detailed during a joint hearing held by the SEC and the CFTC that implied that institutional investors and trading firms had left the market that day as volatility peaked during the session. Senator Schumer said in his letter that any trader or firm making markets in 25 or more stocks or exchange-traded funds should bear trading obligations, according to a draft obtained by Dow Jones Newswires. Market makers were traders who stood ready to take the other side of an incoming order. The SEC must update its definition of market makers to account for the transformation of market making into a competitive industry dominated by computer-driven trading systems, Senator Schumer had said. He proposed requiring such participants to quote prices between the highest bid and lowest offer for a certain period of the trading day, depending on the stock. Market-maker quotes also would need to be "reasonably related" to the current price and not beyond thresholds that would trigger a temporary halt in trading under new circuit-breaker rules, concluded Senator Schumer.[20]

August 24, 2010

In what was to be one of his last communications to SEC chairwoman Mary L. Schapiro, on this date, Senator Ted Kaufman from Delaware urged the agency to review seven stock market practices, saying that developments such as high-frequency trading may erode the confidence of investors. He said that current market structure appeared to be the natural consequence of regulatory structures designed to increase efficiency and thereby provide the greatest benefits to the highest-volume traders; therefore, he added, the agency should analyze the practices "before piecemeal changes" were made that exacerbate the unfairness. Some investors had said computer-driven strategies executing hundreds of trades in a minute make stock prices more volatile and boost costs; NYSE Euronext estimated about 46 percent of daily volume was executed through high-frequency strategies.

Senator Kaufman also asked the SEC to examine dark pools, which matched trades without posting quotes on public exchanges. Dark pools may be "undermining public price discovery," he had said. Finally, Kaufman said that the SEC also should examine the colocation of servers at the exchanges, liquidity rebates paid on the basis of order flow, possible conflicts of interest arising from the disclosure of retail order flow, and how much trading occurred without the involvement of a brokerage firm.[21] Kaufman ultimately was succeeded by Democrat Chris Coons, after Coons defeated Republican nominee Christine O'Donnell in November 2010. Kaufman resigned and left office on November 15, 2010.

August 24, 2010

On this date, Chi-X Europe, the London-based MTF, said that it received a takeover inquiry from an unidentified third party, later identified as BATS Global Markets, which operated the BATS Exchange in North America and BATS Europe, the third-largest venue for trading equities on that continent. Chi-X Europe had become the second most active trading venue for equities, behind the London Stock Exchange. Since 2007, Chi-X Europe had emerged as the primary platform to challenge traditional European exchanges in the wake of adoption of the European Markets in Financial Instruments Directive.

A deal between Chi-X Europe and BATS Europe would unite the two largest stock-trading platforms that emerged after European regulators opened up competition in the industry in 2007, Bloomberg News said. BATS Europe's owners included Bank of America; Citigroup; Inc.; Morgan Stanley; Credit Suisse; Deutsche Bank; GETCO, LLC; JPMorgan Chase and Co.; the estate of Lehman Brothers Holdings, Inc.; Lime Brokerage, LLC; Tradebot Systems, Inc.; and Wedbush Morgan Securities. Chi-X Europe had some overlapping owners, including Citigroup, Bank of America, GETCO, Morgan Stanley, and Credit Suisse. Instinet Holdings, which was owned by Japan's Nomura Holdings, owned 34 percent.[22]

The Impact Is Felt, September–October 2010

Flash orders, the capability provided by the exchanges to traders that had been featured extensively in the press, was going the way of the dinosaur. Meanwhile, the press found a great attention-grabbing substitute with the court processes to former Goldman Sachs and Citadel employees.

September 1, 2010

On this date, two electronic exchanges, BATS Exchange and Nasdaq OMX Group, stopped offering so-called flash orders, which were deemed by some people as giving unfair advantage to some investors at the expense of others. The main characteristic of the flash strategy was to take a stock order, after it had been checked against a market's main order book, and "flash" it to a select group of participants, who had just a fraction of a second to act on the order before it was routed to other exchanges to be filled. The practice had helped exchanges build market share but had come under fire from critics who alleged that it gave some participants an unfair advantage. Direct Edge, the exchange that had come up with this implementation, planned to continue offering the service. No wonder, said *Wall Street Journal* reporter Randall Smith, flash orders accounted for about 25 percent of Direct Edge's profit, even though they accounted for only 5 percent of its trading volume.[23]

September 7, 2010

On this date, SEC chairwoman Mary L. Schapiro raised the idea of requiring firms, especially those not subject to "meaningful obligations governing their quoting behavior," to maintain bids and offers for a minimum time before they could be canceled. The agency was looking at how to ensure that the practices of high-frequency firms do not undermine fair and orderly markets, she said.[24]

September 10, 2010

Liquidnet Holdings, Inc., the trading platform used by institutions such as mutual funds to buy and sell large blocks of shares, eliminated 45 employees on this date because of a slowdown in business. The cuts were confirmed by Rich Myers, a spokesman for the New York–based company. Liquidnet, the world's largest independent operator of dark pools, had about 375 employees before the 12 percent reduction. The cuts were company-wide, affecting trading, technology, and transaction processing, he said.

Despite the cuts, Liquidnet had been able to expand its business outside the United States, including launching dark pools in Malaysia, Poland, the Baltics, and Mexico. "We've had another good year," announced John Barker, head of the international division. He said that Brazil was among the countries next on the map, the current thinking being that it would be live probably by April 2011. "So far this year we've added five to six markets, and they've been trading away nicely," concluded Barker.[25]

September 29, 2010

Following $7 billion in redemptions in the month before, quant hedge fund D. E. Shaw & Co. announced on this date that it was cutting 10 percent of its workforce, representing 150 employees across the board, including partners and portfolio managers, as part of a long-term strategic review by the company.[26]

The industry in many ways was hurting as assets continued to decline. The conventional wisdom had been that bigger companies were faring better because investors showed a preference for established companies with enough resources to install solid compliance and administrative programs. However, as the D. E. Shaw layoffs showed, big fund companies were not immune to global industry trends.[27]

September 29, 2010

On this date, testimony in the lawsuit Citadel filed against former employees Misha Malyshev, Jace Kohlmeier, and Matt Hinerfeld shed light on its secretive high-frequency trading business. Kohlmeier, the math whiz who worked for Malyshev at Citadel and then at Teza Technologies, LLC, testified about the types of problems he tackled in helping to develop the high-frequency trading technique. The group's first task was to build a historical market data system and develop trading signals called *alpha models*, according to a chart on Citadel's business entered into evidence. "Alpha models give you an idea: will something move up or move down?" Kohlmeier said. "Models just produce numbers, not decisions, so someone needs to have a strategy, someone who can turn those numbers into decisions." Trading in the market gave traders "feedback" on the performance, which, in turn, they used to improve the system, he said.

Malyshev, who was born in a rural town in central Russia and came to the United States to study mathematics, eventually ending up at Princeton University, said that the concept of using computer programs to predict share prices is "easy to understand," at least at first. "You start with something simple, and eventually, it becomes extremely sophisticated." He compared it to a living organism. "It needs to be continuously updated to be successful," he said. The computer system's speed, he said, was key to its success. "Number one will get the trade; number two will get nothing," he said. "We were smaller than competitors but the fastest in the world."[28]

October 19, 2010

On this date, Chris Gair, the Jenner & Block's attorney representing Mikhail Malyshev, the former executive with Citadel, confirmed that his client had paid a $1.1 million fine for breaching a court order to preserve documents tied to the legal battle with his former employer. Malyshev and Jace Kohlmeier became embroiled in a court fight last year with the Chicago-based hedge fund firm, which charged that the men violated noncompete agreements with Citadel as they set up a new high-frequency trading firm called Teza Technologies, LLC.

Malyshev acknowledged in court testimony that he deleted files from his home computers even after receiving an order to preserve documents. He was ordered to pay some of Citadel's legal fees and costs associated with analyzing the machines. A monetary penalty of $1.1 million related to that issue was handed down by Judge Mary Rochford, although Citadel requested that the payment be split between two charities, the Greater Chicago Food Depository and the Coordinated Advice and Referral Program for Legal Services.[29]

From the flash crash to the Waddell & Reed trade that started it all, from the discussion about stub quotes to circuit breakers, from the launch of new exchanges in the United States to GETCO's dark pool in Europe, by November 2010, high-frequency trading was on the minds of everyone in the financial world.

CHAPTER 12

Meet the Speed Traders: Manoj Narang

"Nobody can really get an edge over anyone else in terms of proximity these days because colocation is available to whomever wants it. The only way to have a competitive advantage is to have software, systems, or data analysis capabilities [superior to] your competitors."

In 1999, Manoj Narang, founder and CEO of the eight-month-old company Tradeworx, was pitching the company to an audience of venture capitalists attending Red Herring's Venture Market East conference in Cambridge, Massachusetts. Back then, Tradeworx was developing a suite of online financial analysis tools for use by individual investors and was seeking a fresh round of financing.

Fast-forward to May 10, 2010, four days after the so-called flash crash. The *Wall Street Journal*'s Scott Patterson wrote: "For a crucial set of players—high-frequency trading hedge funds—all this turmoil was becoming too risky to handle. One fear that would prove all too real was that in the extreme swings, some, but not all, trades would later be canceled, leaving [trading firms] on the hook for unwanted positions. Narang, whose Tradeworx, Inc., firm runs a high-frequency trading operation in Red Bank, New Jersey, began to worry that the extreme volatility could lead to painful losses in his fund. At about 2:40, he and a small team of traders scrambled to close the positions held by the high-speed fund, which trades rapidly between stock indexes and the individual stocks in the index. Normally, it takes about a fraction of a second to unwind the trades because of the high-powered computers Mr. Narang uses. But, as the market plunged, it took about two minutes—an eternity in today's computer-driven market."[1]

The Man Behind Tradeworx

Narang was born in India and emigrated to the United States with his parents when he was three years old. His parents wanted him to be a doctor, which is probably what sparked him to do something else.

Narang attended public schools in New Jersey. He then went to Massachusetts Institute of Technology (MIT) and majored in math and computer science. His first work experience was during high school as a stock boy and cashier at Walgreen's. After college, he had a number of job offers to work as a programmer in Silicon Valley, but he ended up being intrigued by an offer to work on the trading floor at First Boston in New York City.

"Despite my strength in English, math, and computer science, I had never taken a single finance, economics, or statistics class in college, so I knew nothing about markets or trading when I first got hired to work on the trading floor. When I was getting started, the most appealing thing about trading was that in this profession one is (at least conceptually) judged based on an objective and meritocratic criterion—one's P&L [profit and loss]. I say conceptually because in real life there are many traders who have made millions of dollars in bonus money over their careers, even though the aggregate P&L they have generated over their career is negative. This is so because bonuses get paid annually, which leads to all kinds of suboptimal risk-taking behavior by traders.

"The job at First Boston was the start of a nine-year career on Wall Street, where I worked in technology, research, and trading. In my first trading job, I worked as a bond trader for Citibank, which was, at the time, a primary dealer in U.S. Treasuries. I was not particularly good at the job, which was better suited for people who were previously professional gamblers, fighter pilots, or other such things. To give myself a fighting chance, I designed a trading system that essentially automated my job, and in the process, it discovered all kinds of riskless arbitrages in the broker screens that human traders could not detect. That was my very first experience with high-frequency trading, way back in the mid-1990s. Then, in 1999, I left Wall Street for good to start Tradeworx."

Narang is very frank about the current prospects of a career in high-frequency trading. "It is not a great career choice, longer term. Most of the people who try it fail. It is almost impossible to be competitive without having access to the resources of a large firm, such as advanced technology, low commissions, and top-tier rebates. The regulators are doing their best to make it impossible for smaller players to be competitive. More important, most of the money in this business is still made by long-term professional investors. If one has the skills required to be competitive in the high-frequency trading space, one could have a pretty big impact in some other line of work."

Tradeworx: The Intersection of Finance and Technology

Narang founded Tradeworx in 1999 with the goal of democratizing the role of advanced technology in the financial markets. Tradeworx also operates a quantitative hedge fund business that currently manages hundreds of millions of dollars in assets, as well as an in-house proprietary trading business focused on high-frequency trading strategies.

The transition from chief of a cash-strapped startup to visible leader of the high-frequency trading movement marks a singular turn of events for Narang, the Wall-Streeter turned entrepreneur. What did it take for Narang to start his high-frequency trading operation?

"A massive amount of expertise in trading, market structure, and technology developed and honed over the course of many years. The capital requirements are rather small by comparison. If one has a small edge owing to one's skills in building trading systems or statistically analyzing data, one can translate that into a slightly better than 50 percent winning percentage on every trade one does. For example, say that one has a 52 percent winning percentage. This is pretty much useless if one does one or two trades; however, if one does a thousand such trades in a single day, one can pretty much be sure that around 520 of them will be winners and around 480 of them will be losers. In other words, one's aggregate activity will be profitable even though barely over half of those individual trades are themselves profitable.

"The larger the number of trades one does in this fashion, the more certain one can be that exactly 52 percent of them will be winners. In other words, the margin of error around 52 percent gets smaller and smaller as the sample grows. Mathematically, this is known as the 'law of large numbers,' and it explains why one can make money so consistently with high-frequency trading.

"Tradeworx trades U.S. equities and eventually will expand to all other electronic markets. Like most high-frequency trading firms, Tradeworx doesn't accept external capital because the capital requirements are very low. The main use of outside capital in the world of high-frequency trading is to fund research and development (R&D) and operations, not to actually trade the capital. Very little capital is required for trading purposes.

"Tradeworx is a technology firm, so improvements in our technology happen naturally as a matter of course. We generally are buyers of hardware and builders of software and systems, so the buy-versus-build decision is pretty straightforward. We have around 30 people in the firm, around 25 of whom are involved with high-frequency trading in some capacity. The majority of these are programmers. We recruit exclusively from universities and, with rare exceptions, only hire people with no prior financial industry experience. In order to identify top talent, we put candidates through a very extensive battery of technical evaluations to assess their aptitude in math and computer science.

"Regarding our performance, it is quite good; we have never had a losing week since we started in the business. Usually, the only reason we have a down day is because we are constantly launching new strategies, and it takes time to get them right. We use very little leverage because high-frequency trading strategies are not capital-intensive."

The Impact of Frequency on High Frequency Trading

The *frequency* in high-frequency trading refers to the average rate of portfolio turnover exhibited by a trading strategy. It is an objective quantity related to the ratio between a strategy's trading volume and its average gross holdings, for instance, a strategy that bought and sold $1 million of stock during a trading day and whose average portfolio during the trading day also was $1 million. In order for this to be true, this strategy must have bought $1 million at the open and sold $1 million at the close. Obviously, this strategy has a holding period of one day, meaning that it "turns over" its portfolio once per day. On the other hand, if the strategy did the same amount of volume but only held an average of $100,000 worth of stock at any given time, then the turnover would be 10 times per day.

"Profitability can have two distinct meanings in the realm of high frequency, and these meanings are almost mutually exclusive. When applied to high-frequency trading, *profitability* usually refers to the consistency of profits, because consistency is what makes high-frequency trading so appealing. A successful high-frequency trading strategy generally will have a Sharpe ratio that is higher than 4, and a successful high-frequency trading operation that runs multiple high-frequency strategies generally will have a double-digit Sharpe ratio. Such high Sharpe ratios are unheard of in traditional investment styles.

"To get this high level of consistency, you must exploit the 'law of large numbers,' which is the most fundamental principle of statistics, to the maximum possible degree. This means making as many independent bets as possible within a single trading day. In order to do this with a finite set of tradable securities, you must turn your positions over very quickly. So the most *consistently* profitable high-frequency trading strategies therefore are the ones that have the shortest holding periods.

"However, to most people, profitability means something entirely different, which is the overall *amount* of profit generated. In this regard, the highest-turnover strategies are at a decided disadvantage. It is fairly easy to understand why this is the case. Suppose that a strategy holds a stock for only one minute, on average. Well, a typical stock will move by only a penny or two during a typical one-minute period. Let's say that this strategy has a 55 percent winning percentage on individual trades (this is a pretty good winning percentage for a quant strategy) and that the typical winner is the same size as the typical loser. Then the net winning percentage is 55 percent minus 45 percent, or 10 percent. So one is talking about 10 percent of a 2-cent move as the average profit on a trade, and that is *before* trading commissions, Securities and Exchange Commission [SEC] fees, and other trading costs. By the time all is said and done, one is looking at a profit margin of around 0.1 cent per share on a typical ultra-high-turnover strategy. And that only includes trading costs, not the costs of running such an expensive and technology-intensive business to begin with!

"Just how much money is a tenth of a cent per share? Well, for the past three years, the market has averaged about 8 billion shares per day of volume. If one assumes that high-frequency trading overall does 8 billion shares per day of volume at 0.1 cent per share of profit, that comes to $2 billion of profit in a year. This might sound like a lot of money, but let's keep in mind this is the total amount for an *entire industry*. There are many other corners of the financial industry, such as derivatives trading or hedge funds, that generate hundreds of times this amount of profit in one year.

"In general, these two elements of profitability, consistency versus magnitude, are distinctly at odds with each other. Not only is this intuitively obvious, as I just explained, but it is dictated by the laws of risk and reward. One can follow either a low-risk, low-reward strategy, which gives small profits and a very high Sharpe ratio, or a high-risk, high-reward strategy, where one has the potential to either hit a home run or strike out.

"I don't see more traditional investment managers expanding into high-frequency trading because there is simply not enough profit or capacity to allocate capital for it to be meaningfully profitable. Traditional managers should be focused on investing, *not* on liquidity provision. High-frequency trading is *not* an investment activity. It is like brokerage; it provides a valuable service to investors, but that doesn't mean that investors should seek to become brokers either!"

Liquidity and High-Frequency Trading

In his "Tradeworx, Inc., Public Commentary on SEC Market Structure Concept Release" document, Narang defined *liquidity* as the immediate availability of transactable shares at a fair price. He also established high-frequency trading as the liquidity backbone of the market. In fact, it provides immediacy and fair pricing. By *immediacy*, Narang explains, market makers provide immediately transactable shares at prevailing prices. *Fair pricing* refers to the fact that statistical arbitrageurs will ensure that the information is propagated efficiently from securities being affected by long-term investors to other securities that are correlated, resulting in cross-sectionally fair prices.

"All markets require the existence of firms that specialize in the provision of liquidity to long-term investors. There are two principal ways for this to occur. The old-fashioned way is for the market to designate certain privileged players as dealers of securities. Invariably, these privileges endow dealers with information or capabilities that ordinary investors don't and can't enjoy. Because of this, such markets are known as 'two-tiered markets' because there is not a level playing field between market makers and other traders.

"A newer approach that has become possible because of electronic trading is to decentralize market making by opening it up to competition and empowering all market participants with the same information and capabilities. In such markets, skill rather than status becomes the main determinant of which players have an advantage. No market better exemplifies this meritocratic approach than today's U.S. equity market.

"Nobody should expect market makers to provide their services for free. However, it has been amply demonstrated in practice that markets that have decentralized market makers trading competitively on a level playing field with other traders are the markets that have the lowest transaction costs and the greatest liquidity for investors. Dealer markets, by contrast, tend to be cash cows for Wall Street, which is why the Street opposes exchange-based trading of derivatives.

"People are often confused about the value of the capital markets and their role in the economy. One often hears politicians and regulators claim that the purpose of the stock market is to serve the so-called capital-formation function for corporations, thereby efficiently allocating capital where it is needed. However, this is not strictly true. That is the purpose of the *primary* market, where companies issue their shares to the public and receive cash in exchange. In the stock market, when you buy shares of a stock, you are not buying them from the company itself, so the company does not receive cash from this transaction.

"The stock market is the 'secondary market' for corporate equity securities. As such, its sole purpose is to provide liquidity for investors in the primary market. Because their holdings are liquid, investors are willing to pay a premium to participate in the primary market, which results in greater ability for corporations to raise more cash.

"Thus the main feature one should wish to see in the stock market, in order for it to serve its stated purpose, is *liquidity.* This is precisely the function served by high-frequency traders. By this reasoning, long-term investors are much less important to the capital-formation process than liquidity providers are."

The Speed Challenge for Long-Term Investors

Do investors need to invest in high-performance-trading infrastructure to be competitive? This was the question Narang answered in his response to the "SEC Market Structure Concept Release." He argued that a high-performance infrastructure would allow a long-term investor to focus on opportunities that come and go in a fraction of a second but that such investors instead should be focused on opportunities that unfold over weeks, months, or years. Moreover, he argues, spending bundles of money on high-performance execution creates benefits or efficiencies that can be measured in basis points (1/100 of a percent) or, more typically, in fractions of a basis point.

Narang explains that it is worthwhile for high-frequency traders to invest in such an infrastructure because the resulting improvement in execution quality, though minute, is of the same order of magnitude as the profit margin of high-frequency trading itself. By contrast, an investment in such technology would allow a long-term investor to improve his or her returns from 10 percent (hypothetically) to 10.005 percent. "This is a pointless and stupid exercise given that third-party solutions are available that provide most of the benefit for little or no cost!"

"Retail investors simply don't have the cost structure to profit from high-frequency trading. At the lowest-cost brokerage firm, it still costs several cents per share to place an order. These brokerage fees alone are 10 to 100 times the profit margin of a typical high-frequency trade. More important, one needs to understand that even though the market-making function in equities is decentralized, it doesn't mean everyone should be a market maker. Just because everybody needs food doesn't mean that everyone should become a grocer. Similarly, individuals should seek to be investors, not liquidity providers.

"I see that institutional investors will feel compelled to invest in high-performance trading capabilities if for no other reason than to satisfy their customer base and to be able to tout a competitive advantage over their peers. However, for the large firms that manage billions of dollars, the profits of high-frequency trading will not move the needle enough for them to make the effort to acquire the expertise and capabilities."

Controversy and Misconceptions

The fact that high-frequency traders use low latency, colocation services, and ever-expensive technology to apparently gain an unfair advantage in the markets has created quite a bit of controversy about their behavior.

"There are many reasons for the controversy, but the most important is that the public and policymakers alike are poorly informed on how markets actually work. Also, the financial press has done a very poor job of providing the public with actual facts and instead has fanned the flames by overhyping the issue and airing the grievances of all kinds of self-interested parties.

"There are too many misconceptions around high-frequency trading on the part of the media and the public to name them all. One glaring misconception is that high-frequency trading generates massive profits for Wall Street. First of all, Wall Street has very little to do with high-frequency trading, and second, as I described earlier, the profits are actually very modest (which is the whole reason why Wall Street has very little interest in high-frequency trading). People have the misconception that high-frequency trading practitioners have a kind of "cowboy mentality" and that the markets are like the Wild West as a result. Nothing could be further from the truth. High-frequency traders are among the most responsible and risk-averse players in the market. They have never been implicated in any sort of wild risk-taking behavior, which is quite a contrast from the Wall Street traders who nearly brought the global economy to total collapse in 2008.

"High-frequency trading provides a valuable service to the market and earns a relatively tiny profit in return. Let's consider this: when an individual investor executes a 200-share order in his or her online brokerage account, the investor pays the broker 5 cents per share to execute the trade. The broker does not risk any of its own capital to do this; all the broker does is route the order to the exchange or to a market maker. The player on the other end who actually provides a fill for the trade is a high-frequency trader. The high-frequency trader not only risks his or her own capital to provide the required liquidity but, in exchange, receives only about 1⁄50 of the compensation that the broker (who takes no risk whatsoever) makes on the very same trade. If people have a grievance with the financial establishment, they should ask their brokers why they need to earn 50 times the amount that the liquidity provider earns despite the fact that they are not even risking any capital on the trade!"

Would High-Frequency Trading Be Contributing to Systemic Risk?

"I think the main risk in the financial markets is that capital is getting increasingly concentrated, which makes herdlike behavior ever more prevalent. The frequency with which bubbles inflate and explode is getting more and more rapid as a result because massively capitalized investors jump from asset class to asset class, leaving devastation in their wake. All this has absolutely nothing to do with high-frequency trading.

"There is no exponential growth in high-frequency trading. This is yet another misconception. In any market, market makers should account for roughly half the volume because they should be the typical counterparty for every trade done by a long-term investor. All market making is high-frequency trading, and it always has been. The only pattern of growth is the rate at which fully automated market makers are replacing human market makers in markets that have recently gone electronic. Once a market goes electronic and impediments to trading are removed, it doesn't take long for computers to take over the market-maker function. In the U.S. equity market, this happened a long time ago, and there is no further 'growth' in high-frequency trading as a proportion of overall volume.

"People who talk about 'systemic risks' posed by high-frequency trading don't have any idea what they're talking about. The only systemic risks to the market are the ones posed by herd-like behavior among *long-term investors.* Long-term investors are the ones who inflate asset bubbles when they crowd into the same investments at the same time (such as tech stocks in the late 1990s, real estate in the 2000s, and precious metals today), and they are the ones who cause these bubbles to burst when they all stampede for the exits at the same time.

"Once you're successful, once you have a system that's making money, you become very secretive, because it's very easy for one of your guys to leave and replicate it. What are the exact ingredients and proportions of Coca-Cola? Is there something wrong going on at Coca-Cola? This is the point. It's replication, ease of replication. The barriers to entry, to competing, are not too high."

Tradeworx and other firms like it use such algorithms in the lightning-quick trading approach that is altering the landscape of U.S. markets, driving broker-dealers out of business, and changing how money managers invest. Tradeworx started high-frequency trading in January 2009 and later in the year accounted for about 3 percent of overall volume in the exchange-traded fund SPDR Trust, which tracks the Standard & Poor's (S&P) 500 Index and is one of the most heavily traded securities.[2]

The Importance of Low Latency

The relative importance of low latency for a high-frequency trader depends on what sort of trading he or she does. For some high-frequency trading strategies, latency is not a major issue. To understand why, one has to understand a little bit about how high-frequency trading strategies work, says Narang. High-frequency trading is a form of "statistical arbitrage" that seeks to exploit the fact that markets and securities have semi-stable correlations with each other and that these correlations are sometimes disturbed by the liquidity demands of long-term investors. Correlations arise for structural reasons and for systematic reasons. Structural correlations exist, for example, between indexes and their members. On the other hand, systematic (or statistical) dependence between securities occurs because stock prices have many common underlying drivers (such as interest rates, currency prices, and economic growth rates), so that when an underlying driver experiences a change, the change affects many stocks similarly, explains Narang.

"The importance [the distinction betwen structural correlations and systematic correlations] lies in the fact that structural correlations are very stable over time and hence very easy to model statistically. As a result, when a structural opportunity arises in the market, all quants can identify it, so there is very heavy competition for those opportunities. This means two things: (1) one needs to be faster than the competition if one is going to succeed in accessing the opportunity, and (2) these opportunities tend to be very small and disappear very quickly because it is very easy to arbitrage them out of the market.

"By contrast, most of the money in statistical arbitrage comes from systematic correlations rather than structural ones. Systematic correlations are much trickier to model because they vary over time. Because of the difficulty in modeling such opportunities, they can go undetected for large periods of time before they are deemed to be large enough to be statistically significant. Furthermore, it is highly unlikely that two competing firms modeling the same phenomenon will generate a signal at precisely the same time because the models will be sufficiently different from each other to prevent this from happening. As a result, low latency is not really important at all for such strategies.

"For our strategy, speed is very important. Proximity to the exchanges is one element of the overall speed equation, but it is far from the only step. Nobody can really get an edge over anyone else in terms of proximity these days because colocation is available to whomever wants it. The only way to have a competitive advantage is to have better software, systems, or data-analysis capabilities than your competitors."

Narang's response to the "SEC Market Structure Concept Release" included a section on order anticipation as regulatory arbitrage.

"Regulators need to recognize the difference between *fair* and *unfair* practices related to order anticipation. Using publicly available data more intelligently than your competitors is a *fair* practice, even if the goal is to predict their behavior! Indeed, Tradeworx sees no order flow other than what every other market participant can see on the exchanges' feeds.

"How do I see our fund in five or ten years? I have no idea; five or ten years are an eternity when you are immersed in a world where microseconds matter!"

The Future of High-Frequency Trading

Ciamac Moallemi, assistant professor at Columbia Business School, wrote in the school's blog, *Public Offering:* "Equity markets have changed dramatically in recent years, with the proliferation of electronic trading and the decentralization of trading across many new venues. While these changes have offered investors many benefits, there may be unintended consequences, such as the momentary breakdown that occurred on May 6. This event highlights exactly how little we know about the complex and highly interdependent systems that constitute the market."[3]

How complex and independent the financial markets are can explain why the joint report by the staffs of the SEC and the CFTC on the May 6, 2010 events didn't include any specific recommendations about what needed to be done to avoid a similar event. For Narang, when somebody changes the rules of a complex system, even slightly, it can have a massive effect on the market structure and on the efficacy of certain trading strategies. Moreover, some of those changes can have great unintended consequences, warns Narang, upending entrenched players and setting off new battles for supremacy.

Narang highlights the particular situation high-frequency trading faces, where lawyers make the rules and engineers exploit them. He thinks the engineers will win that battle every time. The current wave of interest in high-frequency trading was catalyzed by the adoption of Regulation NMS (or Regulation National Market System) in 2007. That wave is just now starting to ebb, he says: "Virtually anything the regulators do at this point will serve as a new catalyst and result in a renewed focus on high-frequency trading."

"The media have done a tremendous job of scaring otherwise sane people into believing that they need to buy into the 'arms race' in order to be competitive. Thus I think that in the future we will see a 'mainstreaming' of some of the tools and techniques used by high-frequency traders, meaning that many long-term investors will seek out these capabilities so that they are not at a putative 'disadvantage.'

"A related point is that the financial markets have always been early adopters of disruptive technologies, including the telegraph, the Internet, and high-performance computing. However, these sorts of speed-based advantages are always fleeting. The rest of the market always catches up. In relatively short order, the focus of traders will revert back to generating alpha rather than obsessing over speed.

"I think we're near the end of the arms race, barring further actions by the regulators. When speeds get down to the level of microseconds, the differences in performance between competing firms get narrower and narrower, to the point where the edge becomes unreliable. Thus it will quickly get to the point (if it hasn't already) where the arms race will fizzle out because the incremental speed improvements are just not worth the cost to obtain them."

CHAPTER 13

The Future of High-Frequency Trading

As is the case with many new industries, high-frequency trading slowly emerged in the global financial landscape and then quickly got engaged in controversy, not bearing much responsibility for it, though. What didn't get lost was that high-frequency trading was just a new means to achieve alpha, the perennial goal of any investment manager; while many rules were still in debate, the underlying power of technology was helping entrepreneurial minds and corporate visionaries to reach new heights—small steps if we are to look at this evolution 50 years ahead.

New Regulation Sets In, October 2010

Evolution doesn't happen as smoothly as most market participants would want. While floor traders have become part of financial history, many of them realized the changes happening and transformed themselves in the locomotive of progress not only in the United States but also across the globe.

October 21, 2010

On this date, Chi-X Global, Inc., the electronic trading platform that had won preliminary approval to become a competitor to Australian stock exchange operator ASX, Ltd., said that it was working toward starting operations by March 2011. The company was "eagerly" waiting for the Australian Securities and Investments Commission to publish a new timetable for the entry of rivals to ASX, Peter Fowler, Chi-X Australia's CEO, said.[1]

October 21, 2010

On this date, Singapore Exchange Limited (SGX) made U.S. market-making firm GETCO Asia a trading member of its securities market. Admission of the firm brought the number of trading members on SGX's securities market to 28, following the addition of Cantor Fitzgerald in September 2010. GETCO, which trades on more than 50 markets in the Americas, Europe, and Asia, was already a registered market maker on U.S. exchanges Nasdaq, New York Stock Exchange (NYSE) Arca, and BATS Exchange and had designated market-maker status on European trading venue NYSE Euronext.[2]

October 25, 2010

On this date, SGX said that it was making an $8.3 billion cash and shares takeover offer for the operator of the Australian bourse, aiming to vault from second-tier stock market to leading Asian finance center. The combined exchange company would be the world's fifth largest by market value and rank and the second-largest stock market in Asia by number of listed companies, the two exchanges said in a joint statement. By other measures, the new exchange still would rank behind Tokyo, Hong Kong, and Shanghai. The deal aimed to give both exchanges a better chance of prospering amid increased competition within Asia and as cross-border trading platforms such as Chi-X Europe usurped the dominance of established stock exchanges.

The Australian Securities Exchange, Ltd., known as ASX, was set to lose its monopoly on operating a stock market in Australia in 2011, and an affiliate of Chi-X Europe was planning to set up a trading system once the monopoly was abolished. Singapore, meanwhile, had long lagged behind Hong Kong and Tokyo as a regional financial center.

November 3, 2010

The U.S. Securities and Exchange Commission (SEC) voted to bar brokers from granting high-frequency traders unfiltered access to an exchange, a move aimed at imposing safeguards meant to prevent bad trades from disrupting the markets. "Naked access" let high-speed traders and others buy and sell stocks on exchanges using a broker's computer code without requiring them to filter through the broker's systems or undergo any pretrade checks. Such trading arrangements had exploded with the growth of high-frequency trading firms, which relied on trading speed to make their money and didn't want to be bogged down by a broker's controls.

In some cases, reported the *Wall Street Journal*, brokers relied on assurances from traders that they had their own controls in place. Roughly 30 percent of market activity was conducted through naked access, said John Jacobs, director of operations of Lime Brokerage. The vote would have little impact on the largest high-frequency trading firms because they were broker-dealers who had their own direct access to the markets. It would hurt smaller shops because they would either see their trading slowed down or would need to shoulder the expenses that come with becoming a broker-dealer; broker-dealers have to maintain net capital equal to the greater of $250,000 or 2 percent of aggregate debit items. Mutual funds and other investors that don't rely on trading speed to make their profits would be largely unaffected by the new rules, said Alison Crosthwait, director of global trading strategy for Instinet."[3]

According to James Leman, principal of Westwater Corp., the regulation about naked or sponsored access was just enforcing something that was morally supposed to be enforced in the past anyway. He explains, "When I was enabling buy-side customers to electronically connect to Salomon Brothers, we built monitors, we built tools, and we interviewed them for the kind of trading they were going to do, but even then we didn't appreciate the kind of Gatling gun we were giving our customers; even the exchange didn't require an agreement, but we required an agreement. And we had the ability to establish a daily limit of trading, and we would talk to the investor if he or she got close to it. But the regulation at this point in that dimension says to someone that you are responsible because the rules say that you have to be an agreeing member to gain access to the market, so if you are giving somebody the right to use the pipe, you've got to know what the person is doing because he or she can bring the system down financially, and you are responsible for him or her."

Leman adds: "Because problems also can occur in pedestrian ways, the buy-side guy is using an order-management system or maybe he is using a proprietary thing he has designed himself. Those things are changing people to put enhancements in those systems; they all do regression testing the way they should, to know what is going on, plus the brokers are giving these guys the algorithms, and the guys are changing the algorithms, so you have a lot of potential failure points as well as servers rolling over as well as speed issues, and even exchanges having to close. And the speed issues are picking up; I have had a guy call me up and say that there is something wrong with my system, and it is not my system; it is the order management system he was using. He launched 5,000 orders, but I didn't see them yet; they didn't hit my server. Just because they changed status on his screen, he thinks that he is covered. How granular you have to get, a lot of people don't think through the right way, and now the Gatling gun is an AC-130U Spooky with an amazing fire power; some people don't understand that if everybody shows up at the party at the same time, it gets really interesting, and that's what a lot of the big firms are worried about because they were entitling all the customers, but they weren't gating it; the only people who ever tried to gate it were the exchanges when they adopted different kinds of rules for program trading and individual order flow, and I don't even think those are still in place because they have their other circuit breakers in some places."

November 8, 2010

On this date, the SEC decided to ban stub quotes, which were singled out for blame in the May 6 "flash crash." These were place-holding price quotes, far from the market price, put up by market makers that are required to post quotes but really do not want to buy or sell shares. "While we continue to look at other potential obligations for market participants, this is an important step in our effort to improve the functioning of the U.S. markets and restore investor confidence following the events of May 6," said Mary L. Schapiro, SEC chairwoman.[4]

November 9, 2010

The *New York Times*' Graham Bowley exposed on this date that since the Dow Jones Industrial Average fell about 700 points and then largely recovered on May 6, similar flash crashes have occurred with alarming frequency in more than a dozen individual stocks, setting off circuit breakers intended to halt trading of a stock for five minutes if its price changed by 10 percent within a five-minute period and thus to stop panic from spreading.

The *New York Times* reported that to some analysts, these mini–flash crashes were a sign that another big one is possible, if not probable. Others said these abrupt reversals simply were the way modern, lightning-quick markets work and that investors had better get used to it. An SEC official said that the agency was closely watching the cases where individual stocks had set off circuit breakers but had found that each case had "its own story." The official added, "We are learning from them, and so far it is hard to extrapolate too much as to the general trends in the market."[5]

November 9, 2010

On this date, Assistant U.S. Attorney Thomas Brown said that Samarth Agrawal, former SocGen trader, had stolen the French bank's proprietary computer code for its high-frequency trading business in hopes of using it to build a duplicate system at another firm, secretly printed out copies of the bank's "closely guarded" computer code, and planned to use it to build a copy of the bank's trading program at a competitor, Tower Research Capital, LLC. Brown, the prosecutor, said that SocGen protected its high-frequency trading code like Coca-Cola Co. protects its recipe for its soft drink or KFC guards its recipe for chicken.

However, Ivan Fisher, Agrawal's lawyer, said that Agrawal hadn't stolen anything and had been asked by his manager to work at home on a way to coordinate trading between two high-frequency trading programs. After questions were raised about how much time he was spending in the office on weekends, Agrawal's manager gave him permission to work on projects from home, Fisher said.[6]

November 11, 2010

Chi-East, a joint venture between Chi-X Global and Singapore Exchange Limited (SGX), was launched on this date as the first pan-Asian independent dark pool to be backed by a regional exchange. Many overseas brokers, including Instinet, ITG, Morgan Stanley, Credit Suisse, Citigroup, and BNP Paribas, operated Asian crossing networks or dark pools in which they matched up client order flow away from the public markets, but Chi-East was the first independent, or non-broker-sponsored, alternative dark pool to go live in the region.

Chi-East was widely regarded as a landmark in the development of the Asian equities markets, which were experiencing their first wave of alternative liquidity and competition, a phenomenon that had already transformed both the U.S. and European markets. Chi-East was the first alternative Asian trading venue to aggregate liquidity across borders, offering trading in Singapore, Hong Kong, Australian, and Japanese stocks on an offshore basis. This made it an important trading venue for overseas brokers wishing to trade a number of Asian markets.

Gan Seow Ann, chairman of Chi-East and president of Singapore Exchange Limited, said: "With this launch, Chi-East is leading the way in introducing innovative trading platforms to the region. This reinforces our strategy of attracting new types of market participants and catering to the changing demands of our customers."[7]

Further Fallout from the Flash Crash, November 2010

Agrawal and Aleynikov were permanently added to this history of high-frequency trading and not exactly as the super programmers they longed to be.

November 18, 2010

Trading firms noticed a discrepancy in the times their orders often took to go through different entryways to the same U.S.

stock exchanges, an issue that was prompting increasing concern at a time when the cost to connect to exchanges was only going up. On Wall Street, trading speed was a paramount focus even for firms that were not labeled "high frequency" because the number of clock ticks from the time a trader sends an order to the time an exchange receives it could mean the difference between buying a stock at an intraday low and buying the stock after a rebound that significantly lifted its price.

In turn, trading firms kept a close eye on latency, a measure of time delay. And in monitoring their latencies from one point to the next on an order's path to execution, some firms noticed that with all other conditions equal, orders can take a disparate amount of time to get through separate order-entry ports on the same exchange. Such ports provided access for market participants to enter orders on the exchanges. "We monitor these port statistics closely and may sometimes make decisions about allocation of trading based on these differences," said Mike Beller, chief technology officer at Tradeworx on this date. While Tradeworx and other firms used enough ports that they could easily compare the differences, some trading firms that might need only one or two trading sessions using the ports had been buying more ports from the exchanges to give them more to compare and choose from. Increases in the fees exchanges charged to use their order-entry ports have only added to trading firms' frustration with the latency discrepancies.[8]

November 19, 2010

On this date, former SocGen trader Samarth Agrawal, who surprisingly had admitted at trial that it was wrong for him to have copied the French bank's speed-trading computer code, was found guilty of trade secrets theft by a jury; the panel took two hours to return the verdict against Agrawal after a two-week trial in U.S. District Court in Manhattan.

Agrawal faces a possible prison sentence of up to five years and deportation from the United States. He had been arrested on April 19, the day he was to start a new job to help build a high-frequency trading system at hedge fund Tower Research Capital, LLC. His trial had taken a turn on Wednesday when he said under questioning from his own lawyer that he knew copying and printing SocGen's proprietary code was wrong.[9]

November 23, 2010

U.K. financial services minister Mark Hoban said in a speech on this date that the government was backing a study of how high-frequency trading may shape London as a financial center over the next decade. "The idea is to help us anticipate changes and provide us with the knowledge and evidence we need to help shape future directives," Hoban added. High-frequency trading has grown sharply over recent years to account for about a third of trading volumes in Britain to about three-quarters of all share dealing in the United States.

The study, the latest in a series of Foresight projects under the umbrella of the government's business department, would look at how to avoid "technology-led economic instabilities." The "flash crash" on Wall Street in May, when the Dow Jones Index went briefly into freefall, also sparked regulatory concerns. A group of experts would help to guide the project, including Andy Haldane, director of financial stability at the Bank of England. The European Union was already looking at whether its core Markets in Financial Instruments Directive (MiFID) share-trading rules should be tightened and is expected to propose legislative changes next year. The project also would look at how computer-generated trading will affect financial stability, share price formation and liquidity, competition, trading costs, and the future role and location of capital markets.[10]

November 24, 2010

On this date, Direct Edge Holdings, LLC, the fourth-largest U.S. equity exchange, announced that it was changing the way it handles flash orders, the split-second requests to buy or sell stock that regulators proposed banning last year. Flash trades had drawn scrutiny from the SEC because they allow participants on a trading venue to see equity orders before they're sent to rival markets. Under Direct Edge's plan, buy and sell requests that were previously flashed would be held for 25 milliseconds while an auction was held to fill them.

"It's a product customers have wanted us to pursue and choose to use every day," said William O'Brien, CEO of Jersey City, New Jersey–based Direct Edge. "Now it's a microauction. We've always prided ourselves on being innovative. It has been enhanced and reborn."

More than 50 platforms competed for orders in the American equities market. All were governed by SEC rules that prevented venues from trading investors' shares at levels inferior to the so-called national best bid or offer available to the public. The flash debate concerned the way market centers competing with one another handled a segment of the hundreds of thousands of orders submitted daily by brokers to automated exchanges. Under the standard, a trading platform may hold an order for less than half a second before sending it to a competitor quoting a better price. For someone to execute against it, he or she must match or improve the price prevailing in the national marketplace at that time. Chicago Board Options Exchange, the market that devised the idea of flash orders for stocks, uses them to allow investors in Chicago to get quicker executions than waiting for a response from companies whose computers are based in New York or New Jersey.[11]

Ultimately, though, and following an SEC decision to review flash crash orders, Direct Edge in early 2011 said that it would drop them altogether. "This decision is consistent with our longstanding position that we would abide by the SEC's rulemaking on this topic, and we believe that now is the appropriate time to be proactive and cease offering" the orders, wrote COO Bryan Harkins in an e-mailed statement.

November 25, 2010

French finance minister Christine Lagarde said on this date that more regulation of high-frequency trading was needed because the majority of effects seem to be negative and lead to artificial moves in markets. "My natural tendency would be to at least regulate it strictly and give regulators the capacity to ban it in exceptional circumstances," Lagarde said. She said a framework for regulation was needed, as well as systems to short-circuit high-frequency operations.[12]

November 29, 2010

On this date, the theft trial of Sergey Aleynikov started in U.S. District Court in Manhattan. Assistant U.S. Attorney Joseph Facciponti said that Aleynikov located a computer server in Germany that wasn't blocked by Goldman's firewalls and secretly uploaded portions of the code in the days before he left the investment bank. Aleynikov wanted to use the code to build a similar trading platform at Teza Technologies, LLC, Facciponti said. However, Kevin H. Marino, Aleynikov's lawyer, said that Aleynikov was only trying to download "open source" code that was used on the trading platform and wasn't owned by Goldman or anyone else. Marino said Aleynikov may have violated Goldman's confidentiality policy, but he didn't commit a crime.

The trial, which could take two to three weeks, was focused on the computer programs used by investment banks, hedge funds, and other securities firms to squeeze more profits from their trading operations. Aleynikov, 40 years old, had been charged with theft of trade secrets and transportation of stolen property and faced up to 10 years in prison if convicted on the most serious charge of theft of trade secrets.[13]

The Way Forward, November–December 2010

What had started in the minds of brilliant entrepreneurs had expanded successfully to all corners of the world. Firms with names that would have been unrecognizable just 10 years before were beating established players in their own game. Both GETCO and Citadel not only were expanding in their original activities but also were acquiring or investing in alternative trading platforms in Europe. Asia was becoming the next big battlefield for exchange operators. Europe was following the U.S. lead in terms of reforming the market structure. Overall, exchanges were competing to attract speed traders to their platforms.

November 29, 2010

The Frankfurt Stock Exchange accelerated its plan to conduct all transactions electronically using the Xetra platform. Electronic trading was increasingly dominating financial markets, bolstered by the proliferation of computerized trading systems, which used mathematical algorithms to power dealing strategies independent of the human hand. Rainer Riess said that Xetra would increase efficiency at the Frankfurt Stock Exchange. Rainer Riess, a member of the management board of the Frankfurt Stock Exchange and managing director of Xetra market development at Deutsche Börse, said that the migration to the Xetra electronic platform would make the market more efficient and reduce financial risks.[14]

The Frankfurt Stock Exchange paved the way for a speedy migration from traditional floor trading to a fully electronic platform for buying and selling shares and bonds. Frankfurt's Xontro floor-based trading system will be replaced by Xetra, a computer-based platform developed by the exchange's operator, Deutsche

Börse, by May 23, 2011. Xetra would later be proposed to merge with Euronext.

December 1, 2010

On this date, Equiduct Systems, Ltd., announced that it traded more than 1 billion euros (U.S. $1.31 billion) in November 2010 for the first time as the alternative trading system (ATS) aimed at retail brokers gathered momentum, the company said. The platform's average daily volume for November was 61.8 million euros, and total volume was 1.35 billion euros, Equiduct said in an e-mailed statement. The system, which didn't have any trades in November 2009, notched up its largest-ever daily volume of 86.2 million euros on November 10.

Citadel, LLC, the $12 billion hedge fund firm founded by Ken Griffin, bought in 2009 a majority stake in London-based Equiduct, an MTF operated by the Berlin bourse. At the time of the deal, Equiduct had yet to take business from traditional exchanges such as Deutsche Börse AG, London Stock Exchange Group, PLC, and NYSE Euronext. In December 2009, Citadel had appointed Peter Randall, credited with bringing ATSs to Europe in 2007, as CEO of Equiduct in an effort to spur growth. Equiduct had since sold a stake to Knight Capital Group, Inc., the largest trader of U.S. stocks, and offered rebates to attract traders.[15]

December 6, 2010

On this date, ASX, Ltd., which was selling itself to Singapore Exchange Limited (SGX), said that a study it commissioned by Access Economics confirmed its view that the deal ultimately was in Australia's interest. A merger of the companies would help Australia to become a financial hub in Asia, as well as potentially lowering capital costs for its companies, according to the report, which was released by ASX.

SGX, partly owned by the city-state's government, required the support of Australian prime minister Julia Gillard's minority Labour government and at least four other legislators in parliament's lower house to approve the cash-and-shares deal. The takeover also confronted numerous regulatory hurdles. The Australian Competition and Consumer Commission was reviewing the merger, whereas SGX's bid faced scrutiny from the Foreign Investment Review Board, the Reserve Bank of Australia, and the Australian Securities and Investments Commission.[16]

According to September data from the World Federation of Exchanges, the combined SGX and ASX exchanges would list companies worth about $1.9 trillion, fourth in Asia behind Tokyo, Hong Kong, and Shanghai. Companies trading on the New York Stock Exchange (NYSE) had a total market capitalization of $12.3 trillion, the most in the world. Combined trading volume of the Singaporean and Australian exchanges was worth about $1 trillion during the first nine months of the year, sixth most in Asia and far behind global leader NYSE, which had volume worth $13.8 trillion in the January-to-September period.[17]

December 7, 2010

"To start a high-frequency trading operation, one better buys and builds what one can't buy around one's core system. After that, it is a matter of personal preference and ability. Generally, it seems most efficient to buy non-profit-making components such as market connectors, databases and feeds, and algorithmic frameworks and to invest in building strategies, models, and proprietary tools around that. This is pretty much across all strategies and markets. At the very high end, where now finally hardware acceleration kicks in, the offerings are still very limited, and some building always will be necessary." That's how Peter van Kleef summarized "How to Get High-Frequency Trading Right the First Time" for attendees of an industry monthly gathering in New York City that featured him and Adam Afshar, president and CEO of Hyde Park Global Investments.[18]

December 8, 2010

"Overhaul of the Markets in Financial Instruments Directive" (MiFID) was published by Michel Barnier, the European Union's internal market commissioner. As noted by *Bloomberg News*: "High-frequency traders face European Union limits on the number of orders they can place, as well as requirements to tell regulators how their computer algorithms work. They would not be allowed to exceed a 'ratio of orders to transactions executed' and to 'notify their competent authority' of the trading strategies they use, under draft EU proposals obtained by *Bloomberg News*. Most high-frequency trading 'is done with algorithms and regulators have to understand what's behind them to be certain there aren't any embedded market abuse practices,' Carlos Tavares, chairman of the Committee of European Securities Regulators, or CESR, said in a Brussels interview on November 29."[19]

The MiFID proposals were taking the form of a consultation document, and market participants would be given until February 2, 2011 to send in responses, after which the commission would present draft legislation the following spring. Although MiFID came into full force only about three years earlier, the fast evolution of trading techniques and technological developments means that regulators felt it was already behind the curve. The directive itself also had been a factor in driving some of the changes.

The review would deal with issues including algorithmic and high-frequency trading, dark pools, broker-crossing networks, over-the-counter derivatives, and commodity derivatives. Many of these areas are technically complex and likely to lead to heavy lobbying campaigns by banks, exchanges, and other market players who are concerned about protecting their existing businesses and, if possible, gaining a competitive edge.[20]

December 8, 2010

The U.S. Senate Committee on Banking, Housing, and Urban Affairs held a hearing on this date on "Securities, Insurance, and Investment." The witness included Mary Schapiro, chairwoman of the SEC; Gary Gensler, chairman of the CFTC; James Angel, associate professor of finance at Georgetown University McDonough School of Business; Thomas Peterffy, CEO of Interactive Brokers; Manoj Narang, CEO of Tradeworx; Kevin Cronin, global head of equity trading for Invesco, Ltd., and Steve Luparello, vice chairman of the Financial Industry Regulatory Authority.[21]

In his prepared remarks, Narang lamented that for the past two years, the public has been treated to endless debate about market structure issues. "Are prices posted by market-makers fair, or are they subject to widespread manipulation? What impact do rebates or elevated cancellation rates have on liquidity? Why is speed important to the business of market-making? How do the equities, options, and futures markets influence and interact with each other? The public should never be forced to accept anecdotal or speculative answers to such questions when definitive answers can be had by analyzing data," he concluded.[21]

December 8, 2010

U.S. regulators should move quickly to set position limits in energy and metals markets required by the Dodd-Frank financial regulation law, CFTC member Bart Chilton noted. "The law provides no such authority for regulators to delay the imposition of these limits; there is no regulatory escape valve," said Chilton in prepared remarks.

The CFTC, which must set position limits for the two markets by mid-January, has yet to unveil proposals for public comment, said Chilton, a Democrat who has called for the agency to consider the measure as soon as possible.[22]

December 9, 2010

On this date, the Netherlands Authority for the Financial Markets (AFM) saw no grounds for restricting the use of high-frequency trading. The AFM sees high-frequency trading not as a separate strategy but as a technique for applying short-term trading strategies that have been in use for years. This assessment would change if high-frequency trading were to be used to implement an illegal trading strategy, but in this respect as well, high-frequency trading would be no different from other trading strategies. The AFM reached this conclusion in its study on the role of high-frequency trading in the European financial markets.

The fragmentation of the European securities markets as a result of changes to the market structure has contributed to the growth of high-frequency trading. With high-frequency trading, trading strategies could be implemented that provide liquidity on various trading platforms and that contribute to more efficient price formation for securities.

The AFM took the view that automated trading methods such as high-frequency trading have increased dependency on complex technical systems. It therefore argued that additional requirements should be set in the European context with regard to operational and risk-management systems used by market participants throughout the trading chain.[23]

December 9, 2010

GETCO, LLC, hired the NYSE parent company's director of options to spearhead its relationships with global exchanges, the big market maker, and high-frequency traders. Edward Boyle, NYSE Euronext's director of U.S. options exchanges, would join other high-profile names hired by GETCO. Boyle would focus on "relationships with exchanges and trading platforms and business strategy development," Chicago-based GETCO said in a statement.[24]

Where is GETCO going? The 11-year-old company that already operated in more than 50 markets in North and South America, Europe, and Asia is following the successful path that awaits all firms that focus on alpha generation. GETCO is still a private company, and it would be difficult to estimate its assets under management. Nevertheless, if there is any similitude, a single firm following quantitative strategies, Renaissance Technologies, was able to accumulate at some point $35 billion among its three funds, highly successful Medallion Fund, Renaissance Institutional Equities Fund, and Renaissance Institutional Futures Fund. To get to that point, GETCO and many other firms mentioned in this book would need to continue producing outstanding results, build strong teams, and institutionalize their growth, both organic and through mergers and acquisitions, to become the asset-management firms of the future.

Conclusion

Where High-Frequency Trading Is Going

Exhilarating inflexion point is an appropriate term to describe where the high-frequency trading industry is at the moment, considering the explosion in the number of new funds being started in recent years (now more than 300) and the increased diversity of strategies implemented by quants and managers. Similarly, interest in the underlying strategies and execution, from hedge funds, private equity firms, institutional investors, alternative investment seeders, and consultants, is at a peak if we were to consider the number of high-frequency trading events held in the world's major financial centers as a proxy.

The year 2010 served as the baptism by fire for the high-frequency trading industry. High-frequency traders started the year in the United States with the not very auspicious labeling as the people threatening to take down the most developed financial markets in the world and an increasing scrutiny from regulators and legislators, until the "flash crash" on May 6. Thereafter, a different narrative slowly but surely emerged and started filtering to the press and to mainstream audiences; first, high-frequency trading, as with any new technology, was evolving and therefore presented opportunities for regulators to review the structure of the market and improve it in light of these new advances;

second, while a few firms might have engaged in improper activities in the past, as in any other financial sphere, most of the people in the industry were genuine and honestly looking to beat the markets through thoughtfully tested strategies facilitated by the evolution of technology; and finally, as the report jointly developed by the Securities and Exchange Commission (SEC) and the Commodity Futures Trading Commission (CFTC) clearly showed, high-frequency trading by itself could not have caused the sudden movements in the markets such as the "flash crash," more closely characterized as a panic reaction from human investors.

Nevertheless, the high-frequency trading industry needs to face significant challenges on its way if it wants to continue to generate alpha and prosper in the long run. Most high-frequency trading firms have been started by single visionaries who have successfully launched novel and profitable strategies with their unique flavors; now firms need to succeed in perpetuating themselves. Team structures and culture need to be instilled so that the next generation of traders and quants at these firms can take over and maintain the work that preceded them. As firms expand their operations and start taking external capital, some of them will need to transform themselves into asset-management organizations, after going through some consolidation of midsized high-frequency firms.

High-frequency trading firms use trading strategies and algorithms that are very different from the traditional long-term investments for which most markets and regulations have been designed. In the United States, the decisions by the SEC to require stock exchanges to hand over real-time market data to regulators, enabling them to reconstruct market events such as the "flash crash" and ban naked access, and to endure additional risk, compliance, and regulatory measures for broker-dealers providing market access went a long way toward this objective. Moving forward, the SEC will continue evaluating the U.S.

market structure through three areas: the performance of the market structure in recent years, particularly for long-term investors; the strategies and tools used by high-frequency traders, such as colocation; and dark liquidity in all forms. Europe will take a bit longer to act because important differences have emerged there on how to further regulate high-frequency trading. Rule changes in the United States and Europe have certainly standardized and accelerated trading, sparked competition among exchanges and alternative venues [electronic communications networks (ECNs), alternative trading systems (ATSs), and multilateral trading facilities (MTFs)] and therefore forced strategic mergers and acquisitions activity, such as the impending mergers of the London Stock Exchange and Canada's TMX Group, and Deutsche Börse and NYSE Euronext.

We are near the bottom in terms of competition based on speed (with most players already leveraging colocation, direct fiber, and hardware acceleration), but the future for high-frequency trading couldn't be any brighter. While there may be regulatory changes that affect the growth of high-frequency trading, the industry will continue growing by expanding into different asset classes and developing markets.

In fact, as U.S. and European legislators and regulators continue pushing more of the world's derivatives and other esoteric products trading onto transparent exchanges, high-frequency trading will stand to reap the fruits of its technology investments mostly in the equity and equity derivative markets. Similarly, long-term investment managers will expand their use of algorithmic tools to execute their transactions.

High frequency has conquered any market where electronic trading is facilitated; practitioners are now looking at India, Brazil, and China as the next frontiers to develop strong equity markets and, thereafter, start trading the plethora of listed instruments that even developed markets have yet to see.

Finally, despite the law of diminishing marginal returns in financial markets, there always will be spreads and inefficiencies for high-frequency traders to take advantage of through the use of ever-smarter technologies such as trading systems based on artificial intelligence. Nevertheless, time after time, traders will strive to achieve what really matters: consistent alpha generation.

Notes

Unless indicated otherwise, the quotes are from interviews held with Adam Afshar, Aaron Lebovitz, Manoj Narang, Stuart Theakston, and Peter van Kleef, and presentations made at Golden Networking Experts and Leaders Forums and business receptions.

Introduction

1. Quotes throughout the introduction from this person are from "High-Frequency Trading Experts Forum 2010," Golden Networking (www.hftexpertsforum.com).
2. *Ibid.*
3. *Ibid.*
4. *Ibid.*
5. "Stock Traders Find Speed Pays, in Milliseconds," Charles Duhigg, *New York Times*, July 23, 2009. Check this link: http://www.newyorktimes.com/2009/07/24/business/24trading.htm. The article appeared online on July 23, evening, and a version of this article appeared in print on July 24, 2009, on page A1 of the New York edition.
6. The Financial Information eXchange ("FIX") Protocol is a series of messaging specifications for the electronic communication of trade-related messages, started in 1992 as a bilateral communications framework for equity trading between Fidelity Investments and Salomon Brothers (www.fixprotocol.org/what-is-fix.shtml).
7. "High-Frequency Trading Experts Forum 2010," Golden Networking (www.hftexpertsforum.com).
8. *Ibid.*
9. "Background Article: Program Trading, Algorithmic Trading, Statistical Arbitrage," *Opalesque*, August 9, 2005.
10. "What Does Quantitative Trading Mean?" Investopedia (www.investopedia.com/terms/q/quantitative-trading.asp).
11. "Algorithmic Trading: What Is It?" *Automated Trader* (www.automatedtrader.net/Algorithmic_Trading.xhtm).
12. *Ibid.*
13. "Proprietary Trading," *Financial Times* (http://lexicon.ft.com/term.asp?t=proprietary-trading).

14. "Statistical Arbitrage," *Hedge Funds Consistency Index* (www.hedgefund-index.com/d_statarb.asp).
15. Cristina McEachern Gibbs, "Breaking It Down: An Overview of High-Frequency Trading," *Advanced Trading*, October 1, 2009.

Chapter 1

1. "Instinet Corporation," *FundingUniverse* (www.fundinguniverse.com/company-histories/Instinet-Corporation-Company-History.html).
2. "What Is the Meaning of Nasdaq?" eHow (www.ehow.com/about_6603813_meaning-nasdaq_.html).
3. NYSE Euronext, Timeline (www.nyse.com/about/history/timeline_regulation.html).
4. Lars Kestner, *Quantitative Trading Strategies: Harnessing the Power of Quantitative Techniques to Create a Winning Trading Program* (New York: McGraw-Hill, 2003).
5. New York Stock Exchange (NYSE), "Designated Order Turnaround (DOT)" *B*eginner Money Investing (www.beginner moneyinvesting.com/html/_designated_order_turnaround.htm).
6. "What Is a Designated Order Turnaround?" *wiseGEEK* (www.wisegeek.com/what-is-a-designated-order-turnaround.htm).
7. David A. Dubofsky and Thomas W. Miller, *Derivatives: Valuation and Risk Management* (New York: Oxford University Press, 2002).
8. "Stock Market Crash of 1987," *Investopedia* (www.investopedia.com/terms/s/stock-market-crash-1987.asp).
9. "BNP Buys Neff," *Futures*, August 1, 1994.
10. "Failed Wizards of Wall Street," *BusinessWeek*, September 21, 1998.
11. Robert J. Shiller, *Brokers, Dealers, Exchanges, and ECNs* (New Haven: Yale University Press, 2009).
12. "Xetra," Investopedia (www.investopedia.com/terms/x/xetra.asp).
13. "Connections in Modern Mathematics and Physics," XIII Geometry Festival (www.math.sunysb.edu/events/simons/index.html).
14. "Wealth Is a Numbers Game," *The First Post*, April 26, 2007.
15. Ian Domowitz and Ruben Lee, *On the Road to Reg ATS: A Critical History of the Regulation of Automated Trading Systems,* International Finance, Blackwell Publishing, 2001.
16. Joseph Kahn, "Goldman Sachs to Acquire Electronic Trading Concern," *New York Times*, July 13, 1999.
17. "SEC Approves Nasdaq Quote Display Plan," *New York Times*, January 11, 2001.
18. "Stock Market Goes Decimal," Infoplease (www.infoplease.com/spot/stockdecimal1.html).
19. Ari Weinberg, "Instinet Looks to Beat SuperMontage," *Forbes*, June 10, 2002.
20. Stephen Labaton, "Nasdaq Wins Battle at SEC on New System for Trading," *New York Times*, August 29, 2002.

21. Aaron Lucchetti, "Firms Seek Edge Through Speed as Computer Trading Expands," *Wall Street Journal*, December 15, 2006.
22. Matt Krantz, "Chicago Mercantile Exchange to Go Public," *USA Today*, December 4, 2002.
23. "Peter van Kleef," *Lakeview Arbitrage* (http://lakeview-arbitrage.com).
24. "Nasdaq to Acquire Brut ECN for US$190 Million," *Domain-b.com*, May 26, 2004.
25. Chris Murphy, "New York Stock Exchange Merging with All-Electronic Upstart Archipelago," *InformationWeek*, April 20, 2005.
26. Philip Boroff and Charles Goldsmith, "Nasdaq Agrees to Buy Reuters's Instinet for $1.88 Bln in Cash," *Bloomberg*, April 22, 2005.
27. "Regulation NMS," Investopedia (www.investopedia.com/terms/r/regulation-NMS.asp).
28. "BATS Receives Funding from GETCO and WEDBUSH," BATS Trading, Inc., October 14, 2005.
29. "NYSE and Euronext in $20 Bn Merger," *BBC News*, June 2, 2006.
30. Alexei Barrionuevo, "2 Exchanges in Chicago Will Merge," *New York Times*, October 17, 2006.
31. "Who We Are," Chi-X Europe (www.chi-xeurope.com/home/who-we-are.asp).

Chapter 2

1. Charles Duhigg, "Stock Traders Find Speed Pays, in Milliseconds," *New York Times*, July 23, 2009.
2. M3 Capital's Web site (www.m3capital.com/index.html).

Chapter 3

1. "GETCO Announces Investment by General Atlantic," General Atlantic, LLC, April 16, 2007.
2. Amy Frizell and James Moore, "Nasdaq to Announce Takeover of Swedish Exchange OMX," *The Independent*, May 25, 2007.
3. "Citigroup to Buy Electronic Stock Trader," Reuters, July 3, 2007.
4. Nandini Sukumar and Matthew Leising, "Nasdaq to Buy Boston Stock Exchange for $61 Million," *Bloomberg*, October 2, 2007.
5. "Markets in Financial Instruments Directive—MiFID" (www.mifidirective.com).
6. Scott Patterson and Serena Ng, "NYSE's Fast-Trade Hub Rises Up in New Jersey," *Wall Street Journal*, July 30, 2009.
7. "TA Associates Announces Investment in RGM Advisors," TA Associates, Inc., January 28, 2008.
8. "Flow Traders secures investment from Summit Partners," Finextra Research 2010, June 5, 2008.
9. Nina Mehta, "As Summer Temperatures Rise, Dark-Pool Volume Climbs Higher," *Traders Magazine*, July 18, 2008.
10. *Ibid.*

11. *Ibid.*
12. Kyle Peterson, "UAL Shares Walloped by New Posting of Old News," Reuters, September 9, 2008.
13. Adam Y. C. Lei and Huihua Li, "Still in the Air: Who Reacts to False Information?" Dillard College of Business Administration and G. R. Herberger College of Business, September 10, 2009.
14. Ianthe Jeanne Dugan, Cassell Bryan-Low, and Gregory Zuckerman, "Citadel Dispels Rumors But Can't Mask a Bad Year," *Wall Street Journal*, October 16, 2008.
15. "Citadel High-Frequency Fund Gained $1 Billion Last Year," *FINalternatives*, October 2, 2009.
16. Lavonne Kuykendall, "Light Shed on Trading at Citadel," *Wall Street Journal*, October 5, 2009.
17. "BATS Exchange Goes Live," BATS Trading, October 24, 2008.
18. "BATS Europe Launch Marks MiFID Anniversary," *The Trade News*, October 31, 2008.
19. Daniel Gross, "Capitalists of the Prairie," *Newsweek*, September 12, 2008.
20. Ann Saphir, "Chaos Theorists: Proprietary Trading Firms Racking Up Huge Profits," *Crain's Detroit Business*, January 26, 2009.
21. "Citadel High-Frequency Head Quits," *FINalternatives*, February 20, 2009.
22. Kerry Massaro, "Goldman Sachs Launches Sigma X Liquidity Pool in Hong Kong," *Advanced Trading*, March 2, 2009.
23. Ivy Schmerken, "Nasdaq Rolls Out Flash Orders to Market Participants as Debate Stirs," *Advanced Trading*, June 2, 2009.
24. "Buy-Side Warned on 'Flash' Order Types," *The Trade News*, July 1, 2009.
25. Susanne Craig and Amir Efrati, "Ex-Goldman Worker Is Arrested," *Wall Street Journal*, July 7, 2009.
26. Andrew M. Harris, Katherine Burton, and Saijel Kishan, "Citadel Group Sues Ex-Executives at Teza for Contract Breach," *Bloomberg*, July 10, 2009.
27. B. Nandini Sukumar, "Citadel to Take Majority Stake in Germany's Equiduct Trading," *Bloomberg*, July 21, 2009.

Chapter 5

1. Charles Duhigg, "Stock Traders Find Speed Pays, in Milliseconds," *New York Times*, July 23, 2009.
2. Jacob Bunge, "U.S. Regulators Seen Moving to Ban Dark Flash Orders Soon," *MarketWatch*, July 28, 2010.
3. Jenny Anderson, "U.S. Proposes Ban on 'Flash' Trading on Wall Street," *New York Times*, September 18, 2009.
4. "U.K. Regulator Scrutinizing High-Frequency Trading," *Bloomberg News*, August 3, 2009.
5. Matt Phillips, "Gone in a Flash: BATS, Nasdaq Drop 'Flash' Orders Today," *Wall Street Journal*, September 1, 2009.

6. Jenny Anderson, "U.S. Proposes Ban on 'Flash' Trading on Wall Street," *New York Times*, September 18, 2009.
7. "Nasdaq OMX Announces INET Next Generation Trading Technology," Nasdaq OMX's Web site (http://ir.nasdaq.com/releasedetailcfm?ReleaseID =407969).
8. Nina Mehta, "Data Centers Not Owned by Exchanges Can 'Tilt' Field, NYSE Says," *Bloomberg Businessweek*, April 29, 2010.
9. Nandini Sukumar, "ICAP Opens Algorithmic Trading System as Demand Grows," *Bloomberg Businessweek*, January 12, 2010.
10. Luke Jeffs, "Chief of Chi-X to Leave," *Wall Street Journal*, February 27, 2009.
11. Melanie Rodier, "LSE Takes Control of Rival Trading Platform Turquoise," *Advanced Trading*, December 21, 2009.
12. "Peter Randall Confirmed as New CEO at Equiduct," *The Trade News*, December 18, 2009.
13. Nandini Sukumar, "Hirander Misra Starts Algorithmic Technology Firm after Chi-X," *Bloomberg Businessweek*, March 14, 2010.
14. Nandini Sukumar, "BATS Europe Boosts Speed of Trading in Push for Market Share," *Bloomberg Businessweek*, February 9, 2010.
15. "MiFID Review to Include High-Frequency Trading—Commission," *The Trade News*, February 26, 2010.
16. Shani Raja and Marion Rae, "Chi-X Wins Approval to Open Rival Australian Exchange," *Bloomberg Businessweek*, March 31, 2010.
17. Shani Raja, "Australian Stock Exchange System to Cut Trading Times," *Bloomberg Businessweek*, February 18, 2010.
18. Ayai Tomisawa, "Chi-X Plans Asia Growth but Sees Hurdles," *Wall Street Journal*, August 2, 2010.
19. Chikafumi Hodo, "As Trade Heats Up, Tokyo Bourse Gets Turbocharged," Reuters, January 3, 2010.
20. "Chi-X Japan Passes (Yen) 50 Billion Monthly Turnover Milestone," *Business Wire*, *Wall Street Journal*, December 2, 2010.
21. Richard Teitelbaum, "The Code Breaker," *Bloomberg News*, January 2008.
22. Scott Patterson and Jenny Strasburg, "Pioneering Fund Stages Second Act," *Wall Street Journal*, March 16, 2010.
23. Dan Wilchins, "Renaissance CEO James Simons to Retire: Source," Reuters, October 8, 2009.
24. "High-Frequency Trading Leaders Forum 2010," Golden Networking (www.hftleadersforum.com).
25. Liz Moyer and Emily Lambert, "The New Masters of Wall Street," *Forbes*, September 21, 2009.
26. "SEC Proposes New Rule to Effectively Prohibit Unfiltered Access and Maintain Market Access Controls," Securities and Exchange Commission, January 13, 2010.
27. "High-Frequency Trading Leaders Forum 2010, Golden Networking (http://www.hftleadersforum.com).

28. Liz Moyer and Emily Lambert, "The New Masters of Wall Street," *Forbes*, September 21, 2009.
29. Scott Patterson, "Meet GETCO, High-Frequency Trade King," *Wall Street Journal*, August 27, 2009.
30. "NYSE to Add Global Market Maker GETCO as NYSE Designated Market Maker," GETCO, LLC, February 11, 2010.
31. Kristina Peterson, "Getco To Be GM Market Maker," *Wall Street Journal*, November 15, 2010.
32. "Infinium Capital Management to Absorb Fox River Partners," *Infinium Capital Management* (www.infiniumcm.com).
33. Matt Taibbi, "The Great American Bubble Machine," *Rolling Stone*, April 5, 2010.
34. Chad Bray, "Not-Guilty Plea in Goldman Code Case," *Wall Street Journal*, February 18, 2010.
35. Grant McCool, "US Charges Ex-SocGen Man Over HFT Code Theft," Reuters, April 19, 2010.
36. *Ibid.*

Chapter 7

1. "High-Frequency Trading Leaders Forum 2010," Golden Networking (www.hftleadersforum.com).
2. ITCH is a direct-data-feed interface that allows Nasdaq customers to observe or disseminate information about stock trading activities. ITCH facilitates the display of data concerning added, executed, modified, and canceled orders. It is also possible to exchange cross and stock directory information.
3. OUCH is a digital communications protocol that allows customers of the Nasdaq to conduct business in the options market. With OUCH, subscribers can place, execute, or cancel orders. OUCH allows subscribers to integrate the Nasdaq into their proprietary networks.
4. "High-Frequency Trading Experts Forum 2010," Golden Networking (www.hftexpertsforum.com).
5. Andrew Kumiega and Benjamin Van Vliet, *Quality Money Management: Process Engineering and Best Practices for Systematic Trading and Investment* (New York: Academic Press, 2008).
6. Process Capability Index (www.ehow.com/facts_7530349_cp-cpk-definition-control-chart.html).
7. "High-Frequency Trading Experts Forum 2010," Golden Networking (www.hftexpertsforum.com).

Chapter 8

1. Ivy Schmerken, "Hyde Park Global Bets on Adaptive Models to Trade Arbitrage Strategies in Milliseconds," *Advanced Trading*, September 30, 2009.

Chapter 9

1. "High-Frequency Trading Leaders Forum 2010," Golden Networking (www.hftleadersforum.com).
2. *Ibid.*
3. *Ibid.*
4. Fawn Johnson, "SEC Moves Closer to Eliminating 'Stub Quotes,'" *Wall Street Journal,* May 25, 2010.
5. "High-Frequency Trading Leaders Forum 2010," Golden Networking (www.hftleadersforum.com).
6. "Preliminary Findings Regarding the Market Events of May 6, 2010," report prepared jointly by the staffs of the CFTC and SEC, October 2, 2010.
7. Herbert Lash and Jonathan Spicer, "Waddell Is Mystery Trader in Market Plunge," Reuters, May 14, 2010.
8. Kara Scannell and Tom Lauricella, "Flash Crash Is Pinned on One Trade," *Wall Street Journal,* October 2, 2010.
9. Courtney Comstock, "Read the E-mail an HFT Chairman Is Forwarding Around About the Firm That Caused Flash Crash," *Business Insider,* October 4, 2010.

Chapter 10

1. Michael Kearns, Alex Kulesza, and Yuriy Nevmyvaka, "Empirical Limitations on High Frequency Trading Profitability," *Social Science Research Network,* September 17, 2010.

Chapter 11

1. Joanna Ossinger and Betty Liu, "Gabelli Calls for a Tax on High-Frequency Trading Operations," *Bloomberg Businessweek,* May 12, 2010.
2. Herbert Lash and Jonathan Spicer, "Waddell Is Mystery Trader in Market Plunge," Reuters, May 14, 2010.
3. "Joint CFTC-SEC Advisory Committee on Emerging Regulatory Issues to Meet on May 24," Securities and Exchange Commission, May 17, 2010.
4. Fawn Johnson, "SEC Moves Closer to Eliminating 'Stub Quotes,'" *Wall Street Journal,* May 25, 2010.
5. "High-Frequency Trading Leaders Forum 2010," Golden Networking (www.hftleadersforum.com).
6. Tal Barak Harif, "Goldman Sachs to Offer Algorithmic Trading for Brazilian Stocks," *Bloomberg Businessweek,* May 26, 2010.
7. Julie Creswell, "Speedy New Traders Make Waves Far from Wall Street," *New York Times,* May 17, 2010.
8. "SEC Announces Agenda and Panelists for Market Structure Roundtable," Securities and Exchange Commission, May 28, 2010.
9. Lynette Khoo, "SGX to Boost Trading Speeds, Global Links," *Business Times,* June 4, 2010.

10. Jacob Bunge and Jenny Strasburg, "Citadel Veterans Open Up Own Shop," *Wall Street Journal*, June 9, 2010.
11. "US Exchanges Confirm Four-Month Extension to Circuit Breaker Pilot," *Trade News*, December 11, 2010.
12. "SEC Approves New Stock-by-Stock Circuit Breaker Rules," Securities and Exchange Commission, June 10, 2010.
13. Jonathan Spicer and Rachelle Younglai, "High-Frequency Trader GETCO Hires Key SEC Staffer," Reuters, June 11, 2010.
14. Ann Saphir, "SEC Opens Inquiry After Former Staffer Joins GETCO," Reuters, June 16, 2010.
15. Jeremy Grant, "GETCO Hires FSA's Jennifer Boneham," *Financial Times*, October 5, 2010.
16. "Joint CFTC-SEC Advisory Committee on Emerging Regulatory Issues Announces Agenda, List of Participants for June 22 Meeting," Securities and Exchange Commission, June 21, 2010.
17. "GETCO Makes European Dark Pool Move," Finextra Research, June 25, 2010.
18. "Direct Edge Launches Exchange Operations," Direct Edge ECN, LLC, July 21, 2010.
19. "Direct Edge Launches EDGA, EDGX 'Next Generation' Platforms," A-Team Group, July 21, 2010.
20. Jacob Bunge, "SEC Urged to Tighten Market-Maker Rules," *Wall Street Journal*, August 12, 2010.
21. Joshua Gallu and Michael Tsang, "Kaufman Urges SEC to Review Seven Market Practices," *Bloomberg*, August 24, 2010.
22. Chris Kentouris, "Chi-X Europe's Suitor Reported to Be BATS," *Securities Technology Monitor*, August 24, 2010.
23. Matt Phillips, "Gone in a Flash: BATS, Nasdaq Drop 'Flash' Orders Today," *Wall Street Journal*, September 1, 2010.
24. Nina Mehta, "Stock Orders That Are Canceled Should Spur Penalties, ICI Says," *Bloomberg*, December 8, 2010.
25. "Q & A: John Barker, head of international, Liquidnet," Jeremy Grant, FT.com, December 29, 2010.
26. John Darsie, "DE Shaw, Bank of America (BAC) Layoffs Foreshadow Harsh New Reality for Wall Street," *T3 Live*, September 29, 2010.
27. "D. E. Shaw Layoffs a Sign of Times?" *FierceFinance*, October 1, 2010.
28. Lavonne Kuykendall, "Light Shed on Trading at Citadel," *Wall Street Journal*, October 5, 2009.
29. Jacob Bunge, "Former Citadel Executive Pays $1.1M Legal Penalty to Charities," *Wall Street Journal*, October 19, 2010.

Chapter 12

1. Scott Patterson and Tom Lauricella, "Did a Big Bet Help Trigger 'Black Swan' Stock Swoon?" *Wall Street Journal*, May 10, 2010.

2. Jonathan Spicer and Herbert Lash, "Who's Afraid of High-Frequency Trading?" Reuters, December 2, 2009.
3. Catherine New, "The Risks of High-Frequency Trading," Public Offering, Columbia Business School, May 14, 2010.

Chapter 13

1. Shani Raja, "Chi-X Says It's Working Toward Beginning Australia Operations in March," *Bloomberg*, October 21, 2010.
2. "GETCO Asia Becomes a Member of SGX Securities Market," *Trade News*, October 21, 2010.
3. Jessica Holzer and Kristina Peterson, "SEC Bans 'Naked Access,'" *Wall Street Journal*, November 4, 2010.
4. Graham Bowley, "The Flash Crash in Miniature," *New York Times*, November 9, 2010.
5. *Ibid.*
6. Chad Bray, "Trial Opens for Former SocGen Trader," *Wall Street Journal*, November 9, 2010.
7. Michelle Price, "Chi-East Dark Pool Marks Test Case for Asia," *Wall Street Journal*, November 11, 2010.
8. Donna Kardos Yesalavich, "Concerns Rise Over Speeds, Fees for Exchanges' Order-Entry Ports," *Wall Street Journal*, November 18, 2010.
9. Grant McCool, "Ex-SocGen Trader Samarth Agrawal Found Guilty of Code Theft," Reuters, November 19, 2010.
10. Huw Jones, "Government Sponsors High-Frequency Trading Study," Reuters, November 23, 2010.
11. Nina Mehta, "Direct Edge Adds Share Auction to Flash Orders that SEC Proposed Banning," *Bloomberg*, November 24, 2010.
12. William Horobin, "French Fin Min: Need More Regulation of High-Frequency Trading," *Dow Jones Newswires*, November 25, 2010.
13. Chad Bray, "Goldman Code-Theft Trial Opens," *Wall Street Journal*, November 30, 2010.
14. Joe Morgan, "Frankfurt Stock Exchange Makes Electronic Move," *Deutsche Welle*, November 29, 2010.
15. Nandini Sukumar, "Citadel's Equiduct Says November Trading Passes 1 Billion Euros," *Bloomberg*, December 1, 2010.
16. "ASX Says Report Backs View Merger Benefits Australia," *Bloomberg Businessweek*, December 6, 2010.
17. Alex Kennedy, "Singapore Bourse Makes $8.3B Offer for ASX," *Bloomberg Businessweek*, October 25, 2010.
18. "How to Get High-Frequency Trading Right First Time," High-Frequency Trading Happy Hour, Golden Networking (www.hfthappyhour.com).
19. Ben Moshinsky and Jim Brunsden, "High-Frequency Traders Face European Order Limits," *Bloomberg News*, December 2, 2010.
20. Nikki Tait, "Brussels Plans Overhaul of Market Rules," *Financial Times*, December 15, 2010.

21. "Securities, Insurance, and Investment," U.S. Senate Committee on Banking, Housing, and Urban Affairs, December 8, 2010.
22. Silla Brush, "CFTC'S Chilton Urges Position Limits, High-Frequency Trade Curbs," *Bloomberg*, December 8, 2010.
23. "Netherlands Authority for the Financial Markets Evaluates Use of High-Frequency Trading (HFT) in European Financial Markets," *Mondovisione*, December 9, 2010.
24. Jonathan Spicer, "GETCO Lands NYSE's Options Head in Hiring Spree," Reuters, December 9, 2010.

Index

About the Author

Edgar Perez is widely regarded as the preeminent networker in the specialized area of high-frequency trading. He is chief operating officer of UltraHF Capital, a hedge fund running high-frequency trading strategies, editor for UltraHighFrequencyTrading.com, and founder of Golden Networking (http://www.goldennetworking.net), a premier networking community for business executives, entrepreneurs, and professionals. Golden Networking has been frequently featured in the press, including, *The Wall Street Journal*, *The New York Times*, *Los Angeles Times*, Reuters, and Columbia Business School's *Hermes Alumni Magazine*.

Mr. Perez is host of High-Frequency Trading Happy Hour business receptions in New York City, which draw the world's top industry practioners. He has organized High-Frequency Trading Experts and Leaders Forums in New York City, and High-Frequency Trading Experts Workshops in Hong Kong, New York, Sydney, Singapore, and Mumbai, as well as conferences on subjects as diverse as hedge funds, derivatives, private equity, distressed investing, and China. He has presented at Harvard Business School's 17th Annual Venture Capital & Private Equity Conference and forums organized by Columbia Business School's Career Management Center and Alumni Club of New York.

Mr. Perez has significant experience on Wall Street and in business. He was a vice president at Citibank (2008), a senior consultant at IBM (2006), and a consultant at McKinsey & Co. in New York City (2004).

Mr. Perez has an undergraduate degree from Universidad Nacional de Ingeniería, Lima, Peru (1994), a Master of Administration from Universidad ESAN, Lima, Peru (1997) and a Master of Business Administration from Columbia Business School, with a dual major in Finance and Management (2002). He is a member of the Beta Gamma Sigma honor society.

Mr. Perez resides in the New York City area. He is an accomplished salsa and hustle dancer.

Visit him at www.TheSpeedTraders.com or follow him on Twitter @TheSpeedTraders.